CATALOGUE OF
PAINTINGS AND SCULPTURE AT
DUFF HOUSE

STEPHEN LLOYD

Catalogue of
Paintings and Sculpture at
Duff House

NATIONAL GALLERIES
OF SCOTLAND · EDINBURGH
MCMXCIX

Published by
The Trustees of the National Galleries of Scotland
all rights reserved © 1999
ISBN 0 903598 87 6

Photography by Antonia Reeve
Designed and typeset in Minion by Dalrymple
Printed by BAS Printers
Over Wallop

Front jacket:
François Boucher 1703–70, *L'Aimable Pastorale*, 1762

Back jacket:
John Fleming 1792–1845
*View of Banff with the Bridge over
the River Deveron*

CONTENTS

———

PREFACE

In April 1995 Duff House re-opened to the public after several years of restoration. This great building – designed by William Adam for William Duff, Lord Braco, later 1st Earl of Fife – has taken on a new lease of life. This occurred through a remarkable collaboration between Historic Scotland, who restored the building, and what was then known as Grampian Regional Council and Banff & Buchan District Council, who were paying the running costs. This responsibility was subsequently transferred as a result of local government reorganisation in Aberdeenshire. The National Galleries of Scotland undertook to display throughout the house paintings from the Scottish National Portrait Gallery and the National Gallery of Scotland, as well as incorporating appropriate furniture and decorative arts. Vital loans of tapestries and furniture have been made by the Marquess of Zetland, together with a magnificent group of paintings, graphics, miniatures, sculpture, furniture and decorative arts, that have been loaned by the Trustees of Mrs Magdalene Sharpe Erskine from Dunimarle Castle in Fife.

A fully illustrated guide-book was published in 1995, with support from Mobil North Sea Limited and is now complemented by this catalogue of the paintings and sculpture. This has been written by Dr Stephen Lloyd, Assistant Keeper at the Scottish National Portrait Gallery. The wall plans have been prepared by Charles Burnett, Chamberlain of Duff House.

TIMOTHY CLIFFORD
Director, National Galleries of Scotland

INTRODUCTION

---

*Paintings and sculpture now at Duff House, primarily lent from
the National Galleries of Scotland*

The principal reason why the National Galleries of Scotland involved themselves with the partnership which now runs Duff House, Banff, was to put on public display paintings normally in store in Edinburgh. It was an added attraction to exhibit them well away from Scotland's central belt, which is already well provided with picture galleries, both private and public. Duff House is an architectural masterpiece of European significance. Even though it stands in a relatively unpopulated part of the country, it must have a reason to survive, indeed to perform a function other than as an unoccupied, roofed historic monument. It cried out for pictures of an appropriate history, dignity, and grandeur. The house also required furnishing, but this is the subject of the separate guidebook published in 1995.

The National Galleries of Scotland were aware that James, 2nd Earl of Fife (1729–1809) used the House for displaying his matchless collection of portraits, and so it seemed only fitting to provide somewhat similar contents. We also had a good range of photographs of the principal rooms in the 1870s, which gave a clear indication of how, at least at that time, many of the pictures were selected and grouped on the walls. The current displays reflect this, although not slavishly.

We wanted to furnish Duff House with paintings either by artists of the North-East of Scotland, such as George Jamesone, William Mosman and John Phillip, or of sitters from the North-East, such as *James Gibbs, James Duff of Corsindae*, as well as the Earls of Fife. Finally, we wanted interesting historic images of Duff House and its policies, and of the immediate neighbourhood. Indeed, we have already managed to acquire a few such views, as can be seen on the first floor in Lady Macduff's Dressing Room, the Prince of Wales's Bedroom, and on the second floor in the Study off the Outer Library.

The Scottish National Portrait Gallery also possesses one picture, a handsome portrait of *William Cunningham, 8th Earl of Glencairn* (c.1610–64) by John Michael Wright (1617–94), which formerly hung at Duff House until it was sold in 1907. This has now been returned to the house, and can be seen hanging in the North Drawing Room. The Scottish National Portrait Gallery also owns a fine marble bust of the architect of Duff House, *William Adam* (1682–1731), probably by John Cheere (d.1787), and this too is displayed most appropriately in one of Adam's own masterpieces.

The Scottish National Portrait Gallery has provided other remarkably fitting items from its collections, as with the full-length state portrait of *George II* (1683–1760) by John Shackleton (d.1767), who elevated to the peerage the original owner of Duff House, William Duff, successively as Lord Braco and then as 1st Earl of Fife (in the Irish peerage). We also have on display here from the National Gallery of Scotland Aikman's image of *James Duff of Corsindae* (1678–1762), one of the owner's kinsmen and his factor on his estate at Echt.

William Duff first employed the great Aberdonian architect, James Gibbs, to build him a house – Balvenie – and it is therefore especially appropriate that we have lent a fine portrait of *James Gibbs* (1682–1754) by Andrea Soldi (c.1703 – after 1771). The portrait by William Aikman of *Sir James Campbell of Lawers and Rowallan* (1667–1745) hangs nearby. He also employed Gibbs as an architect, and indeed the handsome aedicular frame over the chimney-piece in the Private Drawing Room, with a *View of Loch Katrine*, also came from Lawers, and the frame was undoubtedly designed by Gibbs. The elaborate painting and gilding of the frame is surely by the firm Norrie of Edinburgh, who worked so extensively at William Adam's other great masterpiece, Hopetoun House.

Throughout the House, visitors may be able to detect or guess why certain pictures have been selected from the National Galleries of Scotland's collections. James Duff, 4th Earl of Fife (1776–1857), distinguished himself as an officer in the Peninsular War, and came back with an interesting group of Spanish paintings. For this reason, we have specially included a fine El Greco of *St Jerome*, and indeed have hung it in the same position as Countess Agnes had her image of *The Christ Child* by Murillo.

We are also fortunate in having on permanent display Fife family pictures – after Francis Cotes (1726–70) of *James Duff, 2nd Earl of Fife* (1729–1806), by Pickersgill after Raeburn of *James Duff, 4th Earl of Fife* (1776–1857), and of *Alexander Duff, 6th Earl of Fife and 1st Duke of Fife* (1849–1912), all on loan from the North-East of Scotland Museums Service. To this rich nucleus of paintings we have been adding engravings and photographs that act as 'footnotes' to expand the visitors understanding of the house, family, and the contents. We hope that, with the assistance of the Friends of Duff House, further appropriate paintings and other works of art will be added by purchase, gift or bequest.

*Being possessed of several good Portraits which belonged to
my family, I began forty years ago, to make additions to
them. I have lately had an opportunity of increasing my
Collection, so that I believe, there are few more numerous.*

*I have always considered the Coins, Medals, and
Portraits, of different ages, as very intimately connected with
the History of the Countries to which they belong. My
Collection of Coins and Medals is very numerous, many of
them rare and in great preservation. To the lovers of History
and the Fine Arts, they must be peculiarly interesting.*

*My chief object, with regard to my Portraits, was to
ascertain the Person represented, the Artist, the date, and the
connexion of the Person with different Families; leaving, in
general, the character and transactions to be gathered from
History and Biography.*

With these words James, 2nd Earl of Fife (1729–1809)
began the preface to his own *Catalogue of the Portraits and
Pictures* in his different houses, although principally those
in Duff House. This catalogue was first published in 1798,
with a dedication to Benjamin West, the President of the
Royal Academy, with a second edition following in 1807.
From this description it is known that, while the Earl
displayed paintings in his other residences at Delgaty
Castle (81 works), Rothemay House (145), Innes House
(98) and Fife House in Whitehall (78), the prime collection was presented at Duff House (336). This made both
the collection of painted portraits as a whole, and in
particular at Duff House, one of the most important in
Britain. The quantity of the portraits at Duff House was
such that when in 1796 Sir William Musgrave compiled
his list of the painted portraits in this house as part of his
great project to record all such representations 'of
distinguished persons in various Public Buildings and
Capital Mansions in England and Scotland', the number
of portraits he recorded at Duff House was only exceeded
by those listed at Knole in Kent, Welbeck Abbey in
Nottinghamshire and Newbattle Abbey near Dalkeith.

James Duff was the son of William, Lord Braco and 1st
Earl of Fife (1697–1763), who commissioned William
Adam to build Duff House. In 1754 James Duff was elected
MP for Banff and continued to be re-elected throughout
the rest of his life, also representing the county of Elgin in
the parliament of 1784. He devoted much of his energy to
improving his property and estates, with the result that he
was twice awarded the gold medal of the Society for the
Encouragement of Arts, Manufactures and Commerce.
He held the appointment of Lord-Lieutenant of county
Banff, and he also founded the town of Macduff, the
harbour of which was built at a cost of £5,000.

The 2nd Earl of Fife was also a notable antiquarian,
his interest in his family and in history leading him to
collect coins and medals, as well as prints. However it
was painted portraits that provided him with a lifelong
fascination. As he stated in the introduction to his
Catalogue, he built up his collection from many sources,
especially by gift and through the London auction
rooms, with a number having been smuggled out of
France as a consequence of the Revolution.

The different ways in which pictures came into Lord
Fife's collection can be seen in the following examples of
portraits that were displayed on the first floor. In the
vestibule was a half-length portrait, thought to have been
painted by Federico Zuccaro, of Mary Queen of Scots'
Italian secretary, *David Rizzio*, which had belonged to
Thomas, Earl of Kellie, who acquired it for Lord Fife. In
the same room was a three-quarter length portrait by Sir
Joshua Reynolds of the famous actress, *Mrs Abington in
the Character of Roxana*, which was presented by the
sitter to Lord Fife. In the South-East Drawing Room was
a portrait thought to be by Pierre Mignard of *Madame de
Maintenon*, which was said to be from the French Royal
collection, and which was given to Lord Fife by the late
Earl of Exeter. In the same room was a portrait by Henri-
Pierre Danloux of the *Comte d'Artois, later Charles X*,
who sat for his picture for Lord Fife, and which was
almost certainly painted when artist and sitter were
exiled in Edinburgh.

Still on the first floor in the Dining Room was another
portrait by Reynolds, this time a whole-length of the
famous society hostess, *Jane, Duchess of Gordon*, which
Lord Fife bought from one of Reynolds's posthumous
sales on April 16, 1796. Another whole-length portrait
with a Reynolds provenance was to be found in the
South-East Drawing Room, depicting *Henry VIII*, and
which was said to have belonged to Cardinal Wolsey. In
the same room was a half-length portrait by Pompeo
Batoni of *Edward, Duke of York*, brother to George III,
which had been sent from Rome by the sitter to Lord
Fife. In the South-West Drawing Room was a three-
quarter length portrait by David Martin of *William
Murray, 1st Earl of Mansfield*, the Lord Chief Justice,
which was commissioned by Lord Fife.

On the second floor, known as the 'principal floor', in
the North Bedroom hung a three-quarter length portrait
by Van Somer of *Francis Bacon, Lord Verulam*, which
had belonged to Dr Newton, late Bishop of Bristol. In
Lord Fife's Bed-Chamber was a portrait by Reynolds of
George, Earl of Tyrconnel, who was 'one of Lord Fife's
most intimate Friends', and which was bought at the
artist's posthumous sale on April 14, 1796. Meanwhile, in
the Library there was displayed a three-quarter length
portrait by Gainsborough of the preacher and forger *Dr*

Dodd, which was bought by Lord Fife at the sitter's sale, after he had been executed in 1777.

The 2nd Earl of Fife also appears to have rescued a number of painted portraits, lamenting the fact that at the end of the 18th century they were less popular than prints:

It is surprising how often curious old Portraits are found in places where nobody almost would ever think of looking for them. They are often thrown out of houses for lumber, the name of the Artist and Person represented being unknown, or are sold to pay debts, or to make way for the modern fashion of papering rooms. I know many houses, where very fine Portraits are put up to garrets, and neglected, while their places are supplied with an eightpenny paper.

The *Catalogue* reveals that the portraits and pictures were hung in most of the main rooms on the two main floors. On the first floor they were displayed in the Parlour, and the Vestibule, including Riley's *Dean Swift*, Gibson's *Self-portrait* and Kneller's *Self-portrait*, *Matthew Prior, Alexander Pope* as well as his portrait of *John, 1st Duke of Marlborough*. Here was also shown a portrait of the most bizarre sitter in the collection, Pine's half-length of *Mademoiselle La Chevalière d'Eon de Beaumont* (1728–1810), a notorious French diplomat, spy, freemason and transvestite. The account of d'Eon is not only of interest in itself, but it also suggests the colourful, anecdotal style of the original catalogue entries, which were probably written by Lord Fife himself:

The Chevalier d'Eon. In a Military Uniform, with the Order of the Croix de St. Louis. The Chevalier D'Eon was educated in a College at Paris, and was an Officer of Dragoons. He was sent to St. Petersburgh as a Milliner, to carry on a Secret and particular Negociation between the Courts of Versailles and Petersburg. When he was admitted with his Millinery Goods, he told the late Empress of Russia that he had a Letter for her Imperial Majesty, upon which she bought all his goods. He was also sent to Petersburgh in a public Character, and was always dressed in a Regimental Suit. He was sent to England as Chargé d'Affaires, when the Count de Guerchy was Ambassador, at the Court of St. James's; it was at that time this Picture was painted. During that period also, he had a Dispute with the Count de Guerchy. – Some years after he was discovered to be of the Female Sex. – Upon this he was recalled to Paris; and when at Calais, two Officers of the Police of Paris arrested him, and compelled him to leave his Male Dress, and be dressed like a Woman, to his great disappointment. When she arrived at Paris she abused the Government in her Conversation, and was therefore sent an exile to Burgundy. – After the Revolution in France, she spent her life in England or Ireland, and was found Fencing in many Places on a Stage, for which reason many Families, who would have otherwise protected her, shut their doors against her. – She now lives in Brewer Street [Soho, London] in great Distress. – Three prints of her are in Lord Fife's Portfolio. Half length.

Other notable pictures were to be found in the South-East Drawing Room, where there were portraits of European Royalty; the South-West Drawing Room; the Dining Room, hung with Duff and Fife family portraits; the Red Damask Bed-Chamber and the Great Staircase. On the second or 'principal' floor, portraits were hung in the Large Drawing Room; the South-East Drawing Room, the South-West Drawing Room, which included Medina's *John, 2nd Duke of Argyll*; the North Drawing Room; the North Bedroom; Lord Fife's Bed-Chamber; the Middle South-East Bedroom and the Library, where there could be seen Jamesone's portraits of *George Buchanan* and *Alexander Henderson*.

This great collection of portrait remained virtually intact, until Alexander, 1st Duke of Fife presented Duff House to the burgh of Banff in 1906, which was followed by his removal and sale of 150 pictures, mainly portraits, at auction in 1907.

PAINTINGS AND SCULPTURE LOANED
FROM MRS MAGDALENE SHARPE
ERSKINE'S TRUST, DUNIMARLE CASTLE,
BY CULROSS, FIFE

The other major loan to the house consists of a fascinating group of pictures and other works of art that used to be displayed at Dunimarle Castle, by Culross, Fife. This massive villa, perched on a bluff overlooking the Firth of Forth, is itself an extraordinary building, dominated by a huge circular tower. Inside, it shows evidence of 'the true rise of the barons' wars', which owed much to the antiquarianism popularised by Sir Walter Scott of Abbotsford. The contents of the castle were the historic ancestral collections of the Erskines of Torrie House, Fife, to which additions were made by the last of the family, Miss Magdalene Erskine, later Mrs Magdalene Sharpe Erskine. It is her entire collection, controlled by her Trustees, that has been placed on loan at Duff House for twenty-five years, on the understanding that the collection will be conserved, displayed, and kept secure by the National Galleries of Scotland. All of the pictures and their frames have indeed now been conserved by us.

The Sharpe Erskine collection on loan to Duff House contains an interesting group of Erskine family portraits, which run from the seventeenth to the nineteenth centuries, together with a varied group of Old Master paintings (principally Dutch) and some very rich and splendid Napoleonic furniture.

This collection was the subject of a remarkable, fully-illustrated manuscript catalogue compiled in 1910–12 by its third curator (and Chaplain to the Episcopalian chapel of St Serf's), the Reverend James Harper, Canon of St Ninian's Cathedral, Perth. From Harper's introduction we learn that Dunimarle was bought in 1835 for £5,000 by Miss Magdalene Erskine, and that after settling there she 'became the wife of Admiral Sharpe, and bore henceforth the name of Mrs Sharpe Erskine…the romantic old lady in her senescence married one who had been an early lover – a union which lasted exactly three days and terminated in permanent separation'.

Mrs Sharpe Erskine died at he age of 85 on 1 February 1872, and by her Will all her property was left to Trustees for the purpose of founding and maintaining 'an Institution for the promotion of the study of the Fine Arts – the collection of paintings and other vertû made by herself and her brothers, Sir James and John Erskine, being made the commencement of a fine Art Gallery'. This notable assemblage included Mrs Sharpe Erskine's own collection and those of her brothers and father. The family collection all came from Torrie, nearby, while the majority of the Old Masters were bequeathed to Edinburgh University by her brother, Sir James, and up until 1983 were displayed by the National Galleries of Scotland. Most are now on show at the Talbot Rice Gallery, University of Edinburgh, while many of his bronzes and finest hardstone vases are on loan to the National Galleries of Scotland in Edinburgh. The pictures that were in Sir James Erskine's London home formed part of the Dunimarle collection, as did – according to Canon Harper – 'a good deal of the finest furniture, including the Napoleonic suites … He was with the Duke of Wellington at the debâcle of Napoleon and he had opportunities of acquiring Empire furniture. But he seems to have paid royally for it'.

Most of the Dunimarle pictures are in handsome Empire-style frames, several with frame-makers' labels from Edinburgh. They all belonged to Major-General Sir James Erskine (1772–1825) and were hung in his London house. As a Lieutenant-Colonel he commanded the 2nd Regiment of Dragoon Guards in the Peninsular War under Arthur Wellesley (later 1st Duke of Wellington), and married Lady Louisa Paget, daughter of the 1st Earl of Uxbridge; her brother, later the 1st Marquess of Anglesey, lost his leg at Waterloo.

Sir James Erskine was a keen connoisseur of Old Masters. He bought heavily in Paris in 1816, and continued to collect right up to the end of his life. Sir James was a founder director in 1819 of 'The Edinburgh Institute for the Encouragement of the Fine Arts in Scotland', and according to invoices at Dunimarle he acquired much of his picture collection through Mr Pizzette of 16 Foley Place, London. He bought the pictures attributed to Teniers and Both from J. B. Pascal of Berlin on 7 January 1820, paying 1300 Prussian dollars, and Pignone's *Santa Prasseda* (then attributed to Carlo Dolci) from Siegfried Bendixen at Hamburg on 13 August 1822 for 50 Frédérics d'Or. This picture is now no longer in the Dunimarle collection. It may indeed be identical to a signed Vermeer now in a private collection in the USA. This picture is probably his earliest known work and is a careful copy of an original by Pignone. Immediately after Sir James's death in 1825, the collection was the subject of a valuation by the great dealer, Samuel Woodburn, who also handled Sir Thomas Lawrence's famous collection of Old Master drawings.

A highlight of the Dunimarle collection – now hanging in Lady Macduff's Dressing Room – is David Allan's lively and much-loved painting from 1780 of *A Highland Wedding at Blair Atholl*, which for a number of years was on loan to the National Gallery of Scotland.

TIMOTHY CLIFFORD
Director, National Galleries of Scotland

STEPHEN LLOYD
Assistant Keeper, Scottish National Portrait Gallery

PRIVATE DRAWING ROOM

—

The Private Drawing Room is hung mainly with seventeenth and eighteenth-century portraits, together with a few landscapes.

SOUTH WALL

1 After Sir Anthony van Dyck 1599–1641
Margaret Hamilton, Lady Belhaven
oil on canvas, 63.2 × 52.8 cm

Lady Belhaven was the illegitimate daughter of the 2nd Marquis of Hamilton by Anna, widow of the 8th Lord Saltoun. The portrait paired with Lady Belhaven's is hung in this room (no.10). The pair is based on Van Dyck's double portrait of Lady Belhaven and her husband, a studio version of which is also on display in this room (no.13). *Dunimarle loan*

2 Scottish, eighteenth century
A View of Loch Katrine
oil on canvas, 90 × 113 cm

This painting is enclosed in a rich frame with a broken entablature, which was designed by William Adam for the parlour at Lawers in Perthshire for Sir James Campbell (no.3). NG2614

3 William Aikman 1682–1731
Sir James Campbell of Lawers and Rowallan 1667–1745
oil on canvas, 76.1 × 64.3 cm

The third son of the 2nd Earl of Loudoun, James Campbell was made Lieutenant-Colonel of the Scots Greys in 1708. He enjoyed a distinguished military career and commissioned William Adam to build his house. PG1395

4 Andrea Soldi *c.*1703–71
James Gibbs 1682–1754
oil on canvas, 111 × 87.5 cm

This portrait is signed with Soldi's initials. James Gibbs, born in Aberdeen of Roman Catholic parentage, was the most important British architect of his generation to work in the baroque style. Gibbs built Balvenie house for Lord Braco. The building in the background of this picture is one of Gibbs's masterpieces, the Radcliffe Camera, Oxford. Andrea Soldi was an Italian portrait and history painter, who worked in London. PG1373

WEST WALL

5 Attributed to Gerard Soest *c.*1600–81
William Hay, 4th Earl of Kinnoull d.1677
oil on canvas, 77 × 64.6 cm

With his origins supposedly in Westphalia, it appears that Gerard Soest had established himself as a portraitist in England by 1650, having developed a style quite distinct from his great rival Sir Peter Lely. *On loan from the Rt Hon the Earl of Kinnoull to the Scottish National Portrait Gallery.* PGL364

6 John Shackleton d.1767
George II 1683–1760
oil on canvas, 240 × 148 cm

The son of George I, the sitter was created Prince of Wales in 1714. After quarrelling with his father, he became the centre of the political opposition and on his father's death in 1727, he succeeded to the throne. William Duff, Lord Braco, was raised to the peerage by George II and owned a portrait of the king. The portraitist John Shackleton was appointed court painter to George II in 1749. PG221

7 Thomas Hudson *c.*1701–79
Charles Erskine 1716–49
oil on canvas, 75.5 × 62.2 cm

The Edinburgh-born sitter, a son of the Lord Justice Clerk, Lord Tinwald, practised as a barrister in London. The painter Thomas Hudson was a Devonian, and master of Sir Joshua Reynolds. NG2131

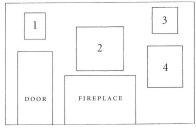

SOUTH WALL · PRIVATE DRAWING ROOM

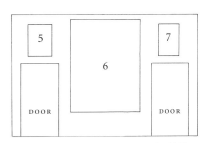

WEST WALL · PRIVATE DRAWING ROOM

8 John Opie 1761–1807
George Dempster of Dunnichen 1732–1818
oil on canvas, 76.2 × 63.5 cm

George Dempster was born in Dundee into a family with a successful trading business, which he inherited while still a young man. In 1761 he was elected a member of parliament for Forfar and Fife burghs. The artist, John Opie, was a Cornishman who was both a portraitist and a history painter. PG2510

9 Attributed to John Cheere 1709–87
William Adam 1689–1748
marble bust, 68.6 cm high

William Adam of Maryburgh held the appointment of King's Mason in Scotland. He was the most prolific designer and builder of houses in Scotland during the first half of the eighteenth century. His reputation as the designer of Hopetoun, Arniston, Haddo and Duff Houses was eclipsed only by that of his sons, John and Robert. PG1033

EAST WALL

10 After Sir Anthony van Dyck 1599–1641
John Hamilton, 1st Baron Belhaven d.1679
oil on canvas, 64.8 × 52.8 cm

Hamilton, created Baron Belhaven in 1647, shortly afterwards took part in the Duke of Hamilton's expedition to rescue King Charles I and was present at the Battle of Preston. Sir Anthony van Dyck came from Antwerp where he had trained in Rubens's studio, later becoming the court portraitist to Charles I. This portrait, together with its pair which is hung in this room (no.1), is derived from Van Dyck's double portrait of Lord Belhaven with his wife, a studio version of which is also displayed in this room (no.13). *Dunimarle loan*

11 French, eighteenth century
James Moray of Abercairny 1705–77
oil on canvas, 76 × 63.6 cm

The sitter was the 13th Laird of Abercairny. This is a copy of a portrait wrongly ascribed to Batoni in a Scottish private collection. *Dunimarle loan*

12 School of Richard Wilson 1713/14–82
View of Wilton House from the South-East
oil on canvas, 54.5 × 90 cm

Wilton House, near Salisbury in Wiltshire, is the seat of the Earls of Pembroke. The popularity of Richard Wilson's interpretations of the Italian countryside helped establish him as the founder of the landscape tradition in British art during the mid-eighteenth century. *Dunimarle loan*

13 Studio of Sir Anthony van Dyck 1599–1641
John Hamilton, 1st Baron Belhaven d.1679, with his wife Margaret Hamilton
oil on canvas, 124.5 × 146.7 cm

Lady Belhaven was the illegitimate daughter of the 2nd Marquis of Hamilton by Anna, widow of the 8th Lord Saltoun. Copies after Van Dyck's two portraits are also displayed in this room (nos.1 and 10). PG1054

14 Cosmo Alexander 1724–72
James Duff of Corsindae 1678–1762
oil on canvas, 77 × 64.5 cm

James Duff settled in Banff during 1700. Signed and dated 1760, this portrait of the eighty-three-year-old sitter hung in his house at Corsindae, which he purchased from William Duff, Lord Braco, on whose nearby estate at Echt he had been factor. The painter was the son of John Alexander, who, after studying in Italy, practised as a portraitist in both Scotland and London, before working in Holland and America. NG2022

15 Italian, eighteenth century
Portrait of a Man
oil on canvas, 81.5 × 61 cm

This portrait was once thought to be by the Venetian painter, Alessandro Longhi. That attribution is no longer convincing. NG1638

16 School of Richard Wilson 1713/14–82
Figures in a Landscape near Tivoli
oil on canvas, 59.5 × 77.8 cm

Tivoli is a famous beauty spot outside Rome and was popular with Grand Tourists during the eighteenth century. Richard Wilson's interpretations of the Italian landscape enabled him to establish an indigenous tradition of landscape painting in Britain. *Dunimarle loan*

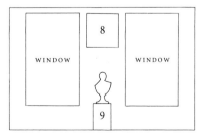

NORTH WALL · PRIVATE DRAWING ROOM

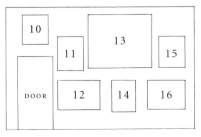

EAST WALL · PRIVATE DRAWING ROOM

CLOSET OFF PRIVATE DRAWING ROOM

———

This closet is hung with a number of works on paper, which are on long loan
from Mrs Magdalene Sharpe Erskine's Trust at Dunimarle Castle by Culross in Fife.
Most were acquired in Italy by members of the Erskine family on the Grand Tour.

SOUTH WALL

1 Neapolitan, 1822
Mount Vesuvius Erupting
gouache, 47.4 × 69 cm
The date of the eruption is inscribed on this work as 26
February 1822. *Dunimarle loan*

2 Domenico Marchetti 1780–*c.*1844 after an unknown
Roman sculptor (no.4)
Female Torso
engraving, 22.1 × 16.2 cm
This was engraved in 1822. *Dunimarle loan*

WEST WALL

3 Neapolitan, nineteenth century
View of the Bay of Naples
gouache, 32.9 × 48.4 cm
Dunimarle loan

4 Roman, first or second century AD
Female Torso
marble, 54.1 cm high
See above (no.2). *Dunimarle loan*

5 Unknown nineteenth-century engraver after
Guariento (di Arpo) fl.1338–67/70
Christ on the Cross
engraving, 44.5 × 28.5 cm
Dunimarle loan

6 Roman, first or second century A.D.
A Man Wearing a Toga
marble, 61.2 cm high
Dunimarle loan

NORTH WALL

7 Elizabeth Erskine
Sir John Drummond Erskine of Torrie 1776–1836
silhouette, 42.5 × 34.5 cm
The sitter was the 4th and last Baronet. Elizabeth Erskine was
one of his sisters. This silhouette was taken in 1803. *Dunimarle
loan*

8 Elizabeth Erskine
Sir William Erskine of Torrie 1770–1813
silhouette, 41.1 × 36.6 cm
The sitter was the 2nd Baronet. Elizabeth Erskine was one of his
sisters. This silhouette was taken in 1803. *Dunimarle loan*

DINING ROOM

The Dining Room is hung with a number of portraits by Allan Ramsay, the finest Scottish portraitist of the mid-eighteenth century. He was the eldest son of the poet Allan Ramsay. After studying in Edinburgh and London, he worked in Italy. In 1738 he established a successful studio in London. In 1767 he was appointed portrait painter to George III. He was chiefly responsible for introducing a new, informal style into British portraiture, which had previously been dominated by the more formal tradition derived from Sir Godfrey Kneller. In the 1750s he turned seriously to literature and in 1754 founded the influential Edinburgh debating club, the Select Society. After 1770 he painted less, devoting himself instead to writing.

NORTH WALL

1 Allan Ramsay 1713–84
James Erskine, Lord Barjarg and Alva 1722–96
oil on canvas, 76.2 × 63.8 cm

James Erskine became an advocate in 1743 and Sheriff Depute of Perthshire five years later, a position he still occupied when he sat to Allan Ramsay for his portrait, which is signed and dated 1750. Made a Baron of the Exchequer in 1754, he eventually became a judge, first as Lord Barjarg and then as Lord Alva. PG2216

2 Thomas Hudson *c.*1701–79
Unknown Gentleman of the Hay Family
oil on canvas, 74 × 62 cm

Thomas Hudson was one of the leading portraitists to fashionable society in London during the middle of the eighteenth century. *On loan from the Rt Hon the Earl of Kinnoull to the Scottish National Portrait Gallery.* PGL358

EAST WALL

3 John Thomas Seton fl.1759–1806
Sir Hugh Paterson, Bt, 1686–1777
oil on canvas, 76.3 × 62.2 cm

This portrait is signed on the reverse and dated 1776. The son of Sir Hugh Paterson of Bannockburn, the sitter succeeded to the baronetcy in 1696 and in 1708 was elected to Parliament as representative for Stirlingshire. PG634

4 Allan Ramsay 1713–84
Patrick Grant, Lord Elchies 1690–1754
oil on canvas, 75.6 × 63.1 cm

This portrait is signed and dated 1749. The son of Captain John Grant of Easter Elchies, Patrick Grant was admitted an advocate in 1712. He collected the decisions of the Court of Session from 1733 to 1757, which were printed in 1813, and he also provided notes to Stair's *Institutes.* PG152

5 Alexis Grimou 1678–1733
Self-portrait as a Drinker ('The Toper')
oil on canvas, 116.5 × 89.5 cm

Grimou was a French portrait painter, although his family was originally from Switzerland. He made a reputation as a portraitist and painter of genre subjects known as *têtes de fantaisie*. A signed version of this self-portrait is in a Parisian private collection. NG664

6 John Vanderbank 1694–1739
James Thomson 1700–48
oil on canvas, 76.8 × 64.1 cm

This portrait is signed and dated 1726. James Thomson was a poet, whose most celebrated work in his own day was titled 'The Seasons'. However 'Rule Britannia', which he wrote in 1740, is now much better known. The painter, John Vanderbank, was born in London, where he spent his whole life and career. PG642

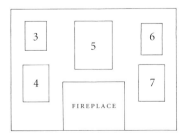

NORTH WALL · DINING ROOM

EAST WALL · DINING ROOM

7 After William Aikman 1682–1731
Susanna Kennedy, Countess of Eglinton 1689–1780
oil on canvas, 73 × 63.1 cm

Susanna Kennedy was the third wife of the 9th Earl of Eglinton, and was a noted patron of letters. William Aikman was the only son of the Laird of Cairnie, near Arbroath. He studied painting under Sir John Baptiste de Medina, and went to Rome in 1707 for three years. He settled in Edinburgh in 1712 and became the finest Scottish portraitist of his generation. *Dunimarle loan*

SOUTH WALL

8 After Francis Cotes 1726–70
James Duff, 2nd Earl of Fife 1729–1809
oil on canvas, 237.5 × 144 cm

The original painting, which is signed and dated 1765 – the year in which it was first exhibited at the Society of Arts in London – is now in the North Carolina Museum of Arts, Raleigh. The painter, Francis Cotes, was a founder-member of the Society of Artists and of the Royal Academy, London. *On loan from the North East of Scotland Museums Service*

9 Manner of Francesco Albani 1578–1660
Polyphemus and Galatea
oil on canvas, 92.5 × 131.5 cm

In classical mythology Galatea was a sea-nymph and the daughter of Nereus and Doris. She fell in love with Acis, who was the son of Faunus (or Pan), although she was pursued amorously by the Cyclops Polyphemus. When he found Acis with the nymph, Polyphemus crushed him with a rock. According to Ovid, Galatea transformed Acis into a river which was then named after him. Francesco Albani was born in Bologna and was a pupil of Annibale Carracci. The picture is probably Roman, eighteenth century. *Dunimarle loan*

10 Allan Ramsay 1713–84
Elizabeth, Mrs Daniel Cunyngham
oil on canvas, 238 × 146 cm

The sitter married Daniel Cunyngham, who lived for a time on the Caribbean island of St Kitts, where he owned extensive sugar plantations. The pose, the costume and the background closely follow Sir Godfrey Kneller's portrait of Margaret Cecil, Countess of Ranelagh, one of his series of Hampton Court 'Beauties' which were painted in 1690–91. This work was probably painted in 1740 or shortly before, around the time of the Cunynghams' marriage. NG2133

WEST WALL

11 George Jamesone 1589/90–1644
Self-portrait
oil on canvas, 28.9 × 23.2 cm

Jamesone, a native of Aberdeen, was apprenticed to John Anderson in Edinburgh during 1612. After the death of Adam de Colone in 1628, Jamesone became the leading portrait painter in Scotland. Horace Walpole referred to him as 'the Van Dyck of Scotland'. PG592

12 Attributed to William Robertson fl.1753–7
Walter Macfarlan of Macfarlan d.1767
oil on canvas, 77.4 × 64.2 cm

This portrait is dated 1757 on the reverse. Walter Macfarlan was the second son of John Macfarlan of Arrochar. From his earliest days Macfarlan devoted himself to antiquarian research connected with the history of Scotland. Formerly attributed to John Thomas Seton, this picture may well be the work of the little-known Edinburgh 'limner' William Robertson. *On loan from the National Museums of Scotland to the Scottish National Portrait Gallery.* PGL34

13 Studio of Allan Ramsay 1713–84
Archibald Campbell, 3rd Duke of Argyll 1682–1761
oil on canvas, 74.3 × 61.6 cm

The 3rd Duke of Argyll was the most powerful political figure in Scotland during the 1740s and 50s. Ramsay painted three different portraits of him, all of which were engraved and much copied. This copy was painted in Ramsay's studio in 1759, possibly by his assistant David Martin. PG908

14 Alexander Nasmyth 1758–1840 after Allan Ramsay
Allan Ramsay 1713–84
oil on canvas, 38.2 × 31.7 cm

The original self-portrait, which is now in the National Portrait Gallery, London, was perhaps painted in Italy around 1737. According to an old inscription on the reverse, this version was painted by Ramsay's pupil Alexander Nasmyth on 26 April 1781. PG189

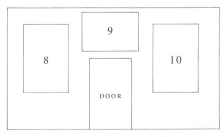

SOUTH WALL · DINING ROOM

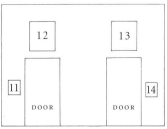

WEST WALL · DINING ROOM

LADY MACDUFF'S DRESSING ROOM

———

Lady Macduff's Dressing Room is hung mainly with seventeenth, eighteenth and nineteenth-century portraits
on loan from Mrs Magdalene Sharpe Erskine's Trust at Dunimarle Castle.

NORTH WALL

1 Dutch, seventeenth century
Unknown Gentleman
oil on canvas, 99 × 74.4 cm

The sitter was aged forty-four when this portrait was painted in 1626. *Dunimarle loan*

EAST WALL

2 John Powell fl.*c*.1780 – after 1833
Stephen Henry Hough c.1776 – after 1828
oil on canvas, 63.8 × 45.7 cm

According to a memorandum written by the sitter in later life, Powell was a drapery painter and finisher working for Sir Joshua Reynolds. This portrait was painted in 1783, when Hough was seven years old, and it was given by the artist to Reynolds, who, apparently, greatly admired it. NG2298

3 Scottish, eighteenth century
Henrietta Erskine 1780–1801
oil on canvas, 37.5 × 30.5 cm

The sitter was one of the younger daughters of Sir William Erskine of Torrie, 1st Baronet (1728–95). *Dunimarle loan*

4 Scottish, eighteenth century
The Hon Colonel John Erskine of Carnock d.1768
oil on canvas, 123 × 99 cm

This portrait was painted by an artist working under the stylistic influence of William Mosman (*c.*1700–71). *Dunimarle loan*

5 Arthur Perigal 1816–84
The Bridge of Alvah
oil on canvas, 68.9 × 95.8 cm

In 1772 James, 2nd Earl of Fife had the majestically arched Alvah Bridge constructed across the chasm of the River Deveron to the south of his estate, and it soon became a well known beauty spot.

Born in London, the painter, Arthur Perigal moved with his artist father to Edinburgh around 1830. *On loan from Historic Scotland*

6 Pierre Falconet 1741–91
Hugh Hume, 3rd Earl of Marchmont 1708–94
oil on canvas, 61 × 50.8 cm

Hugh Hume was a particularly able critic of the Prime Minister, Sir Robert Walpole. In 1744, Chesterfield and Pitt formed their administration, and the sitter commenced an active part in politics. Falconet, the son of the noted sculptor, Etienne-Maurice Falconet, was born in Paris. He came to London in 1766, returning to Paris in 1773. PG1184

7 After Philippe Mercier 1689–1760
Frederick Louis, Prince of Wales 1707–51
oil on panel, 28.8 × 24.9 cm

The eldest son of George II, Frederick is remembered today as the father of George III and as the cause of the greatest scandal of the times – his life-long quarrel with his father and mother. Despite his failings Frederick was popular with the people and gathered round him the leaders of the political opposition. He was also a notable collector and patron of the Rococo. PG964

8 Francisco de Zurbarán 1598–1664
A Young Mother Invoking the Blessing of St Raymund Nonnatus for her New-born Child
oil on canvas, 82.3 × 42.5 cm

St Raymund was known as 'non-natus' because he was delivered from his mother's womb after her death in labour. Thus he was invoked as the patron saint of expectant mothers. This painting and its pendant which represents *St Raymund Reviving a Dead Christian Enslaved by the Moors*, were painted by Zurbarán about 1626. They formed part of an altarpiece dedicated to St Raymund in the Convento del Señor San José in Seville. Zurbarán was one of the greatest painters of the Seville school, specialising in powerful interpretations of religious life in seventeenth-century Spain. *On loan from a Private Collection*

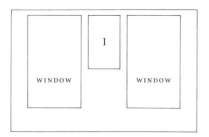

NORTH WALL · LADY MACDUFF'S DRESSING ROOM

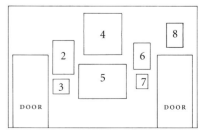

EAST WALL · LADY MACDUFF'S DRESSING ROOM

9 Daniel Gardner 1750–1805
Two Children – Miss Fortescue and her Sister
pastel and gouache, 53.5 × 42.6 cm

Born in Kendal, the artist studied at the Royal Academy Schools, where he came under the influence of Sir Joshua Reynolds. He was particularly known for his fashionable small-scale portraits in pastel and gouache on paper. NG1936

10 French, nineteenth century
Two Spaniels
oil on canvas, 21.2 × 28.8 cm
Dunimarle loan

11 David Allan 1744–96
A Highland Wedding at Blair Atholl
oil on canvas, 102 × 156 cm

The inscription by Allan on the reverse of the painting's lining canvas reads as follows: A HIGHLAND WEDDING / DAVID ALLAN PINXT / AT BLAIR IN ATHOLL 1780 / NEIL GOW FIDDLER / DONALD GOW BASS / MOST OF THE OTHERS FROM NATURE. The picture was painted after Allan's return from Italy, and is the first of his many Scottish genre subjects. Gow was a celebrated violin player, composer and collector of music, whose services were retained by the Duke of Atholl, for a fee of £5 a year. The tartan worn in this picture was done so illegally, for Highland dress had been proscribed after the Jacobite rising of 1745 in an Act not repealed until 1782. *Dunimarle loan*

WEST WALL

12 Circle of William Mosman *c.*1700–71
Unknown Lady
oil on canvas, 63.5 × 53.5 cm

Mosman was possibly a native of Aberdeen, where he died. He may have trained briefly with Aikman in London, but was in Rome from around 1728 to 1732 studying under Francesco Imperiali. By the early 1750s Mosman had established himself as a portraitist in Edinburgh, and during the 1760s he ran a drawing school in Aberdeen. *Dunimarle loan*

13 Scottish, seventeenth century
John Erskine, 2nd (and 7th) Earl of Mar 1558–1634
oil on canvas, 76.4 × 63.2 cm

Lord High Treasurer and Regent, Mar was guardian of Prince Henry Frederick. In 1604 he was created Lord Cardross. A full-length version of this portrait, in which the sitter is wearing Garter dress, and datable to around 1626, is in a Scottish private collection. *Dunimarle loan*

14 Follower of Joseph Highmore 1692–1780
Mrs Stirling of Keir
oil on canvas, 127 × 101.3 cm

Joseph Highmore was one of the major portrait painters working in London during the reign of George II. His development as a portraitist ran parallel to that of Hogarth. *Dunimarle loan*

15 Attributed to David Scougall fl.1654–77
Unknown Lady
oil on canvas, 63 × 52.5 cm

David Scougall was one of a family of painters by that name, who were active in Scotland during the second half of the seventeenth century and the early eighteenth century. *Dunimarle loan*

16 Sir William Beechey 1753–1839
Sir John Drummond Erskine of Torrie 1776–1836
oil on canvas, 75.3 × 63.2 cm

The sitter was the 4th and last baronet. This portrait was painted in 1821. *Dunimarle loan*

17 Circle of Richard Waitt fl.1708–32 after George Jamesone 1589/90–1644
Sir William Wallace c.1272–1305
oil on canvas, 76.5 × 63.5 cm

This picture is a fanciful portrayal of William Wallace, Scotland's great patriot leader of the Wars of Independence. It is based on a painting by George Jamesone, one of the leading portrait painters in seventeenth-century Scotland, whose own self-portrait can be seen in the Dining Room (no.10). *Dunimarle loan*

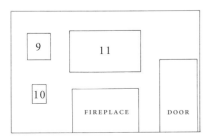

SOUTH WALL · LADY MACDUFF'S DRESSING ROOM

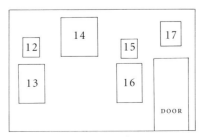

WEST WALL · LADY MACDUFF'S DRESSING ROOM

ORIENTAL CLOSET

―――

1 Toyokuni III (Utagawa Kunisada I) 1786–1864
Three Geishas
coloured woodcut, 35 × 74.3 cm
Dunimarle loan

2 Indian, eighteenth century
A Moghul Horseman
oil on canvas, 17 × 36.7 cm
Dunimarle loan

PASSAGE OFF
LADY MACDUFF'S DRESSING
ROOM

―――

1 Nicolas de Launay after Niclas Lafrensen
(called Lavreince) the Younger 1737–1807
L'Heureux Moment
line engraving, 38.2 × 27.2 cm
On loan from the National Gallery of Scotland

2 Jean Dambrun after François Isidore Queverdo
1741–*c*.1808
La Levée de la Mariée
line engraving, 35.2 × 27.2 cm
On loan from the National Gallery of Scotland

3 Charles Louis Lingée after Sigmund Freudeberger
1745–1801
Les Confidences
line engraving, 38.3 × 29.4 cm
On loan from the National Gallery of Scotland

HUNTING ROOM

—

*This room is hung mainly with seventeenth, eighteenth and nineteenth century
portraits, as well as a notable group portrait by David Allan.*

EAST WALL

1 William Simson 1800–47
A Dog's Head
oil on canvas, 62.5 × 53.1 cm

Born in Dundee, William Simson received his training at the
Trustees' Academy in Edinburgh. He established his reputation
in Scotland mainly as a landscape painter, and in 1829 was elected
to the Royal Scottish Academy. In 1838 he settled in London
where he painted figure subjects. NG708

2 Formerly attributed to James Hamilton *c.*1640–*c.*1720
Still-life
oil on canvas, 47.8 × 40.5 cm

This work bears a false date (1695) and signature of James
Hamilton, a Scottish painter working in the Southern Netherlands and Germany. It may be by Jacobus Biltius (1633–81), a
still-life painter specialising in the depiction of dead
game. NG1833

SOUTH WALL

3 Sir John Watson Gordon 1788–1864
Unknown Lady
oil on canvas, 127 × 101 cm

Sir John Watson Gordon, who became the President of the Royal
Scottish Academy, was the main inheritor of Sir Henry
Raeburn's practice as portraitist to the Scottish
establishment. NG650

4 Attributed to George Scougall fl.1690–1737
Sir Robert Gordon of Gordonstoun 1647–1704
oil on canvas, 73.7 × 62.9 cm

Dated 1692, when the sitter, a man of science, was aged forty-
four. This may be a copy after a work by a member of the
Scougall family of painters, who were active in Scotland at the
turn of the eighteenth century. PG1512

5 William Hamilton 1751–1801
Henry Siddons 1774–1815
oil on canvas, 68.3 × 52.9 cm

The sitter was the eldest son of the famous actress Sarah Siddons,
and he himself went on to become an actor. This portrait, which
was painted in 1783 and engraved two years later, is a reduced
replica from Hamilton's full-length portrait of Henry Siddons
with his mother depicted in the role of Isabella from Thomas
Southerne's play *The Fatal Marriage*. A portrait of his wife is also
hung in this room (no.9). PG1487

6 Jean-Baptiste Oudry 1686–1755
A Dog Pointing to a Pheasant
oil on canvas, 111 × 154.5 cm

Oudry was the foremost animal painter working in France during
the first half of the eighteenth century, specialising in hunting
scenes and depictions of dead game. He was also a notable
tapestry designer, becoming the head of Louis XV's Gobelins
tapestry works. The theme of a dog pointing to pheasants was a
favourite of Oudry's, and in the late 1720s and early 1730s he
painted a series of paintings on this subject as overdoors for Louis
XV's appartments at the Château de Compiègne. *On loan from a
Private Collection*

7 John Russell 1745–1806
Mrs Gumley
pastel, 85.7 × 73.7 cm

This pastel is signed and dated 1777. The son of a book and print
dealer, John Russell became a pupil of Francis Cotes. He
established himself as a fashionable portraitist in pastels, and was
elected an Associate of the Royal Academy in 1772 and a full
Academician in 1788. NG1525

8 Attributed to William Aikman 1688–1731
Unknown Lady
oil on canvas, 76 × 63.3 cm
Dunimarle loan

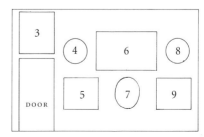

EAST WALL · HUNTING ROOM

SOUTH WALL · HUNTING ROOM

9 John Wood 1801–70
Harriet Murray, Mrs Henry Siddons 1783–1844
oil on canvas, 64.5 × 54.3 cm

Harriet Siddons was married to the eldest son of the celebrated actress, Sarah Siddons. Harriet's most famous role was Diana Vernon, the romantic Jacobite heroine from Walter Scott's *Rob Roy*. PG214

WEST WALL

10 Unknown artist, nineteenth century
Brigadier James Wolfe Murray of Cringletie 1814–90
oil on canvas, 126.8 × 101.4 cm

PG2879

11 David Allan 1744–96
Sir William Erskine of Torrie and his Family
oil on canvas, 153.7 × 240 cm

The family group includes Sir William Erskine of Torrie, 1st Baronet (1728–95), his wife, Lady Frances Erskine (*d.*1793), together with seven of their children, William Erskine, 2nd Baronet (1770–1813), James Erskine, 3rd Baronet (1772–1825), and John Drummond Erskine, 4th and last Baronet (1776–1836), as well as Frances, Henrietta, Elizabeth and Magdalene Erskine. The painter David Allan was the major producer of such 'conversation pieces' in Scotland during the later part of the eighteenth century. This group was painted in 1788.
Dunimarle loan

NORTH WALL

12 George Watson 1767–1837
Mary Augusta Riddell, later Mrs Cunliffe 1823–79
oil on canvas, 143 × 114.3 cm

The artist, George Watson, was born on his father's estate at Overmains, Berwickshire. After studying with Alexander Nasmyth, he went to London where he worked for two years under Reynolds. Watson then settled in Edinburgh, where he established himself as a portraitist and competitor to Raeburn. The sitter was a daughter of Sir James Riddell of Sunart. She and Zoe de Bellecourt (see no.14) were sisters. NG720

13 Follower of Sir John Baptiste de Medina
*c.*1659–1710
The Hon Col William Erskine of Torrie d.1695
oil on canvas, 76.2 × 63.5 cm
Dunimarle loan

14 George Watson 1767–1837
Zoe de Bellecourt, later Mrs Stafford
oil on canvas, 129 × 98.4 cm

The sitter and Mary Augusta Riddell (see no.12) were sisters. NG1885

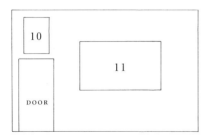

WEST WALL · HUNTING ROOM

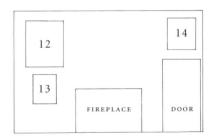

NORTH WALL · HUNTING ROOM

COUNTESS AGNES'S BOUDOIR

―――

This room is hung principally with Italian, Netherlandish and Spanish old master paintings from the National Gallery of Scotland.

NORTH WALL

1 John Alexander 1686–*c.*1766
Colonel William Erskine of Torrie 1691–1754
oil on canvas, 127.5 × 102 cm

John Alexander, a native of Aberdeen, is recorded as working in London during 1710, while in the following year it is known that he painted a self-portrait in Italy. Based in Rome, he executed a number of portraits of the exiled Jacobite court. He returned to Scotland in 1720, establishing studios in Aberdeen and Edinburgh. In 1729 he signed the foundation document for the Edinburgh Academy of St Luke. He was the father of the portrait painter Cosmo Alexander (1724–72). *Dunimarle loan*

2 After Hans Asper 1499–1571
Huldrych Zwingli 1484–1531
oil on panel, 25.9 × 19 cm

According to the Latin inscription, this portrait shows the great Swiss Protestant theologian at the age of forty-eight. Asper, the leading painter in Zurich of his day, is known to have painted a series of portraits of the Zurich reformers in 1550. This work is now thought to be a seventeenth-century copy based on the portrait in the Kunstmuseum, Winterthur. NG1927

3 Henry Bone 1755–1834 after Sir Peter Paul Rubens 1577–1640
An Old Woman and a Boy with a Lighted Candle
enamel on copper, 20.3 × 17.5 cm

The subject may refer to the ancient Greek notion of the wisdom of common life being passed from one generation to another. In a related print an inscription devised by Rubens reads: 'Who is to stop one light being taken from another? A thousand may be taken without any loss to the original.' The implication of this is that talent or knowledge may be passed on without any loss to the provider. The original painting by Rubens is now in a private collection. Bone was one of the foremost copyists in enamel working in London during the late eighteenth and early nineteenth centuries. NG661

4 Attributed to Allan Ramsay 1713–84
Lady Frances Wemyss, Lady Steuart Denham 1722–89
oil on canvas, 127 × 98.4 cm

Lady Frances Wemyss was the eldest daughter of James, 7th Earl of Wemyss. In 1743 she married Sir James Steuart Denham, 4th Baronet of Coltness and Goodtrees. PG2867

5 Netherlandish, sixteenth century
The Virgin and Child
oil on panel, 65 × 50.8 cm

The pose of the Christ Child as well as the Virgin's hands and arms are derived from the lost painting of the *Madonna in the Apse* by Robert Campin, also known as the Master of Flémalle. That particular painting exerted a strong influence on Gerard David and his contemporaries. The facial type of this painting suggests that it was painted by a follower of Gerard David in the early sixteenth century. NG2074

6 Follower of Egbert van Heemskerck 1634/35–1704
Boors Carousing
oil on canvas, 26.5 × 30.8 cm

This painting may be by an English follower of van Heemskerck, who worked in England for much of his career. NG1515

EAST WALL

7 Dutch, seventeenth century
Portrait of a Man
oil on panel, 40.1 × 33.3 cm

This picture was thought to be a self-portrait by the Scottish still-life painter William Gouw Ferguson, who spent the greater part of his career in Holland. NG1832

8 German, early sixteenth century
St John with a Donor and his Sons
oil on panel, 58.5 × 25.7 cm

This picture, together with its pair of *St Andrew with the Donor's Wife and Daughters* (no.13), originally formed the wings of a small devotional triptych. They have both been cut down to their present size, and can be dated to around 1525. The artist was probably working in the Lower Rhine area, close to the Dutch border, and shows the influence of Bartholomäus Bruyn. NG998

9 After Raphael (Raffaello Santi or Sanzio) 1483–1520
The Virgin and Child with the Infant St John the Baptist (The Aldobrandini or Garvagh Madonna)
oil on panel, 29.5 × 22.3 cm

This is one of many versions and copies that were made of Raphael's famous devotional picture now in the National Gallery, London. NG1854

10 El Greco (Domenikos Theotokopoulos) *c.*1541–1614

St Jerome in Penitence

oil on canvas, 104.2 × 96.5 cm

St Jerome is portrayed here with many of his usual attributes: a crucifix, a skull, and an hour glass symbolising the passage of time, together with books and pen and ink denoting his scholarship, as well as the stone, which he clasps, for self-chastisement. His cardinal's hat hangs on a rock to the left. This version, which is one of several, is considered to be one of the two finest examples, and has been dated to around 1600 or just before. The execution may point to it being a good studio repetition. NG1873

11 Polidoro da Lanciano *c.*1515–65

The Holy Family

oil on panel, 42.6 × 52 cm

Polidoro di Paolo di Renzi was born at Lanciano in the Abruzzi mountains in central Italy, but was mainly active in Venice. His style was heavily dependent on Titian, and he specialised in the production of small-scale devotional pictures such as this Holy Family. Similar paintings by Polidoro, which incorporate this pose of the Virgin and Child, are to be found at Raby Castle in County Durham, and in the Museum of Fine Arts in Budapest. An X-radiograph of this painting reveals a female portrait underneath the present composition. NG105

12 Tintoretto (Jacopo Robusti) 1518–94

The Head of a Man with a Red Beard

oil on canvas, 36 × 27.2 cm

Acquired by the National Gallery of Scotland during the last century, this fragment is generally accepted as an autograph early work. It has strong stylistic links with a portrait of a young man in the Kunsthistorisches Museum, Vienna. NG689

13 German, early sixteenth century

St Andrew with the Donor's Wife and Daughters

oil on panel, 58.2 × 26.3 cm

This picture, together with its pair of *St John with a Donor and his Sons* (no.8), originally formed the wings of a small devotional triptych. They have both been cut down to their present size. NG999

14 Follower of Lorenzo di Credi *c.*1457–1536

The Holy Family

oil on panel, 30 cm diameter

This work was originally acquired by the National Gallery of Scotland as by Lorenzo di Credi, although it was soon recognised as a school work. Lorenzo d'Andrea d'Oderigo, known as Lorenzo di Credi, was a pupil of Andrea del Verrocchio. He later ran a busy workshop in Florence, where his designs were reproduced by his assistants. This painting has recently been attributed to an artist known as 'Tommaso', who was strongly influenced by Lorenzo di Credi. NG646

15 Attributed to Adriaen van Ostade 1610–85

An Interior with a Pig's Carcase

oil on panel, 46.2 × 57.9 cm

Born in Haarlem, Ostade was probably a pupil – together with Adriaen Brouwer – of Frans Hals. The peasant genre paintings by Brouwer were an early influence on Ostade, whose best work was of domestic scenes. There is doubt whether the signature is genuine. There is a similar work by Ostade in the Städelsches Kunstinstitut, Frankfurt. NG54

SOUTH WALL

16 Unknown artist, eighteenth century

Frederick II (the Great), King of Prussia 1712–86 and Field Marshal James Francis Edward Keith 1696–1758

oil on canvas, 71.2 × 85.6 cm

James Francis Edward Keith was the younger brother of the 10th Earl Marischal, whose family were strong supporters of the exiled Royal House of Stewart. For nine years he served in the Spanish Army and then changed to the Russian service. From 1728 until 1747 he distinguished himself as a leader of the Russian army in its wars against the Turks and the Swedes but eventually fell from favour. He left Russia and entered the service of Frederick the Great of Prussia. Almost immediately he was made a Field Marshal, and was Frederick the Great's right hand man during the Seven Years War. After sharing in the early victories, Keith was mortally wounded at the Battle of Hochkirch. PG2878

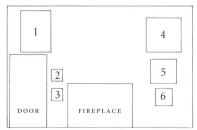

NORTH WALL · COUNTESS AGNES'S BOUDOIR

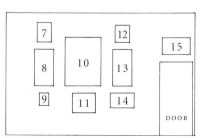

EAST WALL · COUNTESS AGNES'S BOUDOIR

17 Circle of Otto van Veen *c*.1556–1629
The Head of Christ
oil on panel, 48.8 × 38.4 cm

The Netherlandish artist Otto van Veen is best known as the principal teacher of Rubens. *Dunimarle loan*

18 Jan Daemen Cool 1584–1660
A Dutch Family Group (Portrait of Two Boys)
oil on panel, 108 × 83.2 cm

This picture, datable to 1633, was originally part of a larger painting that also included the following fragment with four other members of the family, which is hung nearby (no.19). To the right of this composition a boat is rowing out to a warship, which bears the arms of Rotterdam. During conservation after the Second World War, the removal of a large area of repainting revealed part of a dog, which the artist had painted in two positions. The painter Jan Daemen Cool was a portraitist based in Rotterdam, but the seascape in the distance may have been painted by Adam or Abraham Willaerts. NG824

19 Jan Daemen Cool 1584–1660
A Dutch Family Group (Portrait of a Man, Woman and Two Girls)
oil on panel, 133.4 × 115.6 cm

This fragment, inscribed and dated 1633, is one of two that originally came from a larger painting. The other fragment also belongs to the National Gallery of Scotland and is hung nearby (no.18). NG2259

20 Netherlandish, sixteenth century
Landscape – Midday
oil on panel, 37.2 × 200.2 cm

This landscape has been attributed to various sixteenth-century Netherlandish artists. However, the most plausible candidate suggested to date has been the Antwerp-born painter Jacob Grimmer (*c*.1525/6–90). There appears to be some influence from Venetian art, such as engravings by Domenico Campagnola (1500–64). NG101

21 Imitator of Giorgione *c*.1477/8–1510
A Man Holding a Recorder
oil on panel, 45.8 × 34.9 cm

Bought by Andrew Wilson in Genoa in 1830 on behalf of the Royal Institution in Edinburgh, and then thought to be a self-portrait by Giorgione, this attribution was challenged in the 1930s. NG35

22 Ludolf Bakhuyzen 1630/1–1708
A Coastal Scene
oil on canvas, 48 × 55.6 cm

This work is by one of the finest marine painters working in Holland during the seventeenth century. Based in Amsterdam, he created distinctive pictures in which he stressed the restless action of the waves and dramatic lighting of clouds. *Dunimarle loan*

23 Attributed to Edward Luttrell fl.1680–1724
John Sage 1652–1711
pastel, 33 × 27.3 cm

The sitter, John Sage, was born at Criech in Fife, where his family had lived for several generations. He strongly supported the Episcopalian church party, and was forced to leave his parish by the Presbyterians, who obtained power in 1688. Thereafter Sage wrote in defence of the Episcopalian clergy, who had been driven from their livings. Sage was privately consecrated in Edinburgh in 1705 as a bishop without diocese or jurisdiction. The identity of the artist is not certain but it may well be Edward Luttrell, who was said to have been born in Dublin. PG1848

CORRIDOR

C. Süssnapp and Schenck & Son after Sir Francis Grant
Agnes Georgiana Hay, Countess of Fife (d.1869)
lithograph, 52.5 × 33.8 cm

Daughter of William, 18th Earl of Erroll, and of Lady Elizabeth Fitzclarence (natural daughter of William IV and Mrs Jordan), in 1846 she married James Duff, 5th Earl of Fife.
Acquired by the National Galleries of Scotland for Duff House

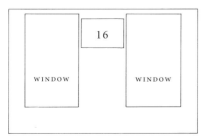

SOUTH WALL · COUNTESS AGNES'S BOUDOIR

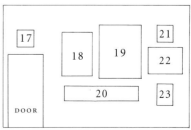

WEST WALL · COUNTESS AGNES'S BOUDOIR

CHINA CLOSET

In the case are a small group of miniatures of the Erskine family on loan from Mrs Magdalene Sharpe Erskine's Trust at Dunimarle Castle by Culross in Fife.

1 Alexander Wellwood Rattray 1849–1902
Mrs Magdalene Sharpe Erskine 1787–1872
oil on canvas, 58.5 × 43.3 cm

Magdalene Erskine was the youngest daughter of Sir William Erskine of Torrie. She and her family can be seen in the group portrait by David Allan, which hangs nearby in the Hunting Room (see no.11). She purchased Dunimarle Castle in 1835 for £5,000, and filled it with her family's collection of fine and decorative arts. After a brief marriage to Admiral Sharpe, she changed her name to Mrs Sharpe Erskine. On her death at the age of eighty-five, all her property was left to be administered by Trustees, for the purpose of founding and maintaining 'an Institution for the promotion of the study of the Fine Arts'. *Dunimarle loan*

2 George Engleheart 1753–1829
Lt Col Sir William Erskine 1729–95
watercolour on ivory, in gold frame, the reverse glazed with pleated hair, in fitted red leather case, 6 cm high

This can be dated to around 1790. An oil painting after this miniature (or no.3) can be seen in the North Drawing Room (no.12). *Dunimarle loan*

3 George Engleheart 1753–1829
Lt Col Sir William Erskine 1729–95
watercolour on ivory, 5.6 cm high

This can be dated to around 1790. A replica miniature by Engleheart also exists in this collection (no.2). *Dunimarle loan*

4 Jeremiah Meyer 1735–89
Unknown Gentleman
watercolour on ivory, 4.4 cm high

This can be dated to around 1775. *Dunimarle loan*

5 Scottish, eighteenth century
Unknown Gentleman
watercolour on ivory in fitted red leather case, 7.8 cm high

This can be dated to just before 1800. *Dunimarle loan*

6 Scottish, nineteenth century
Unknown Lady
watercolour on ivory in fitted red leather case, 8.5 cm high

This miniature can be dated to just after 1800. *Dunimarle loan*

7 Unknown artist, eighteenth century
Unknown Gentleman
watercolour on ivory, set in a brooch, 2.3 cm high

This profile miniature, can be dated to the second quarter of the eighteenth century. *Dunimarle loan*

8 Unknown artist, eighteenth century
Unknown Lady
oil on copper in fitted fish-skin case, 5.8 cm high

This can be dated to around 1740. *Dunimarle loan*

9 Unknown artist, nineteenth century
Unknown Lady
watercolour on ivory in fitted red leather case, 8.8 cm high

This can be dated to just after 1800. *Dunimarle loan*

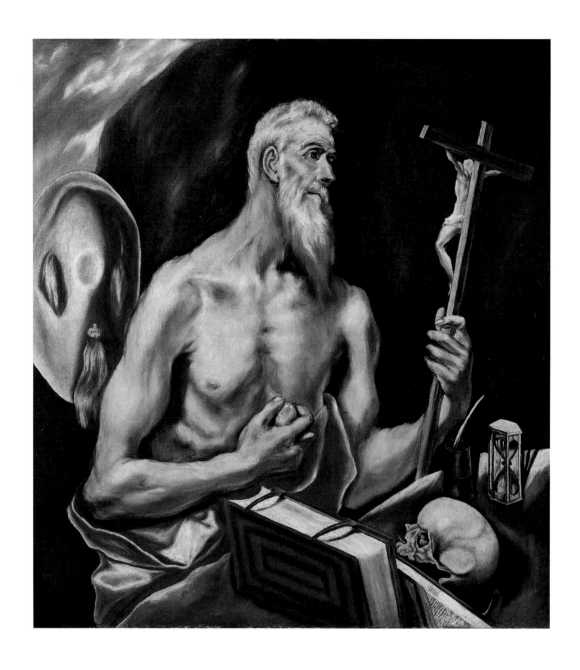

PLATE 3
Henry Bone 1755–1834 after Sir Peter Paul Rubens 1577–1640
An Old Woman and a Boy with a Lighted Candle
enamel on copper, 20.3 × 17.5 cm
NG661 · SEE PAGE 21

PLATE 4
George Jamesone 1589/90–1644
Anne Erskine, Countess of Rothes d.1640, with her Daughters, Lady Mary Leslie b.1620 (later wife of the 7th Earl of Eglinton)
and Lady Margaret Leslie 1621–88 (later wife of the 2nd Earl of Wemyss)
oil on canvas, 219.4 × 135.5 cm
PG2456 · SEE PAGE 35

PLATE 5
Allan Ramsay 1713–84
Elizabeth, Mrs Daniel Cunyngham
oil on canvas, 238 × 146 cm
NG2133 · SEE PAGE 15

PLATE 6
William Delacour fl.1740–67
Sir Stuart Threipland 1716–1805
oil on canvas, 130 × 152.5 cm
PGL354 · SEE PAGE 51

PLATE 7
David Allan 1744–96
A Highland Wedding at Blair Atholl
oil on canvas, 102 × 156 cm
DUNIMARLE LOAN · SEE PAGE 17

VESTIBULE

———

*The Vestibule is mainly hung with seventeenth,
eighteenth and early nineteenth-century portraits on loan from the Scottish
National Portrait Gallery. The room is dominated by one of William Etty's
great subject pictures.*

SOUTH WALL

1 After Salvator Rosa 1615–73
A Figure in Armour
oil on canvas, 87 × 60.2 cm

The subject is based on a figure from Rosa's etched series,
Le Figurine. NG600

2 After Salvator Rosa 1615–73
A Figure in Armour
oil on canvas, 87.5 × 60.5 cm

The subject is based on a figure from Rosa's etched series,
Le Figurine. NG600A

3 Carlo Albacini fl.*c*.1780–1807 and Filippo Albacini
1777–1858 after an unknown Classical sculptor
Augustus Caesar
plaster, 90.3 cm high

NG loan

WEST WALL

4 Thomas Campbell 1791–1858
Sir James Erskine of Torrie, Bt., 1772–1825
marble, 65.2 cm high

This bust of the 3rd Baronet, Sir James Erskine, was sculpted in
Rome in 1823. The sitter, a Major-General in the Peninsular
War under Wellesley (later the 1st Duke of Wellington), was a
major collector of Dutch seventeenth-century paintings, which
he bequeathed to Edinburgh University. Thomas Campbell was
the finest neo-classical sculptor in Scotland. *Dunimarle loan*

5 William Etty 1787–1849
The Combat: Woman Pleading for the Vanquished
oil on canvas, 304 × 399 cm

This remarkable painting, which symbolises the Beauty of
Mercy, was exhibited at the Royal Academy in 1825. It was
bought by Etty's friend, the painter John Martin, who had
rashly promised to buy it for 300 guineas if it failed to sell. The
picture was sold by Martin to the Scottish Academy in 1831.
The National Gallery of Scotland owns four other large-scale
paintings by Etty of Old Testament subjects, including three
scenes from the life of Judith and *Benaiah Slaying Two Lion-
Like Men of Moab*. A smaller finished version of *The Combat*
belongs to the City Art Gallery in York, and a lively oil sketch
on board also survives in a private collection. NG189

6 Thomas Campbell 1791–1858
Sir John Drummond Erskine of Torrie, Bt., 1776–1836
marble, 63.2 cm high

This bust of the 4th and last Baronet, Sir John Drummond
Erskine, is dated 1836. *Dunimarle loan*

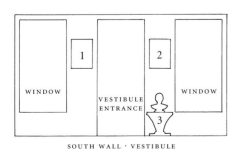

SOUTH WALL · VESTIBULE

WEST WALL · VESTIBULE

7 Attributed to John Scougall *c.1645–1737*
James Maule, 4th Earl of Panmure c.1659–1723
oil on canvas, 75.6 × 62.2 cm

As a young man, the sitter, James Maule, served as a soldier on the Continent, and succeeded his brother George, 3rd Earl of Panmure in 1686. He took part in the Battle of Sheriffmuir and was taken prisoner on the field but was rescued by his brother (see no.11). John Scougall was a member of a family of painters, who were active in Scotland during the second half of the seventeenth century and the early eighteenth century. *On loan from the Rt Hon the Earl of Mar and Kellie to the Scottish National Portrait Gallery.* PGL233

8 Gavin Hamilton *1723–98*
Elizabeth Gunning, Duchess of Hamilton (later Duchess of Argyll) 1734–90
oil on canvas, 67.3 × 55 cm

The sitter, Elizabeth Gunning, was a famous beauty of her day. Gavin Hamilton was born in Lanarkshire. On moving to Rome he turned to history painting, becoming well-known as a member of the neo-classical group which was centred around Mengs and Winckelmann. He also carried out many archaeological excavations in Italy and was an enthusiastic antiquary and dealer. This portrait, another variant of which is in the Scottish National Portrait Gallery, is related to Hamilton's full length portrait of the Duchess at Lennoxlove. PG814

9 After Daniel Mijtens the Elder *c.1590–c.1647*
William Douglas, 8th Earl of Morton 1582–1648
oil on canvas, 76.5 × 63.5 cm

The sitter was Lord High Treasurer of Scotland. PG1858

10 Daniel Mijtens the Elder *c.1590–c.1647*
George Hay, 1st Earl of Kinnoull c.1572–1634
oil on canvas, 215.4 × 134.3 cm

According to the inscription this portrait was painted in 1633 when the sitter was aged 63. Sir George Hay was the fourth son of Sir Peter Hay of Megginch. He was knighted in 1609 and received a valuable patent in the same year for the manufacture of iron and glass in Scotland. Hay was made a Lord of Session and Clerk-Register in 1616, and in 1622 he was made Lord High Chancellor of Scotland. Daniel Mijtens was a Dutchman who came to England before 1618. He was employed by the Court, but was later overshadowed by the arrival of Anthony van Dyck. *On loan from the Rt Hon the Earl of Kinnoull to the Scottish National Portrait Gallery.* PGL189

11 Attributed to John Scougall *c.1645–1737*
Henry Maule, Titular Earl of Panmure d.1734
oil on canvas, 75.2 × 62.2 cm

The sitter was the third son of George, 2nd Earl of Panmure. During the rising of 1715 he joined his brother the 4th Earl of Panmure and took part in the battle of Sheriffmuir where he rescued his brother, who had been taken prisoner (see no.7). He was sometimes styled Earl of Panmure as he would have succeeded his brother, but for the attainder. John Scougall was a member of a family of painters active in Scotland during the second half of the seventeenth century and the early eighteenth century. *On loan from the Rt Hon the Earl of Mar and Kellie to the Scottish National Portrait Gallery.* PGL242

12 John Medina the Younger *1721–96* after circle of Daniel Mijtens the Elder *c.1590–c.1647*
Unknown Gentleman
oil on canvas, 61.5 × 49 cm

This is a copy of a portrait in the National Gallery of Scotland, which was long considered to be a self-portrait of the Scottish painter John Scougall (NG2032). It now appears to be by a Dutch artist of the 1620s, in the circle of Daniel Mijtens the Elder. NG554

13 John Medina the Younger *1721–96* after William Aikman *1682–1731*
Andrew Hume, Lord Kimmerghame d.1730
oil on canvas, 76.2 × 63.5 cm

This painting is dated 1753. PG1554

14 David Scougall *fl.1654–77*
Sir Peter Wedderburn, Lord Gosford c.1616–79
oil on canvas, 77.4 × 64.8 cm

During the Civil War and the Commonwealth, the sitter, Peter Wedderburn, remained firmly attached to the Royalist cause and at the Restoration he was knighted and made Keeper of the Signet for life. In 1661 he was appointed clerk to the Privy Council and in 1668 he was raised to the bench as an ordinary Lord of Session, taking the title Lord Gosford from the estate of that name, which he purchased in 1658. He was regarded as an eloquent advocate and an upright judge. David Scougall was one of a family of painters, who were active in Scotland during the second half of the seventeenth and early eighteenth century. PG1583

15 David Martin *1737–98*
Revd Robert Henry 1718–90
oil on canvas, 76.5 × 63.5 cm

In 1774 Robert Henry was elected Moderator of the General Assembly. His *History of England* was published between 1771 and 1793 in six volumes. It enjoyed great popularity, running through several editions and was translated into French. The painter, David Martin, was the son of the parish schoolmaster of Anstruther in Fife. He became a pupil of Allan Ramsay, whom he accompanied to Rome, and later studied at St Martin's Lane Academy in London. He returned to Scotland with a reputation as a portrait painter, and divided his practice between Edinburgh and London. *On loan from the National Museums of Scotland to the Scottish National Portrait Gallery.* PGL37

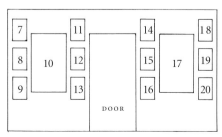

NORTH WALL · VESTIBULE

16 John Medina the Younger 1721–96 after
Sir Godfrey Kneller 1646–1723
John Hamilton, 2nd Baron Belhaven 1656–1708
oil on canvas, 76.2 × 63.5 cm

During the debates in the Scottish parliament leading up to the
Act of Union, the sitter, Lord Belhaven, sprang to fame with his
eloquent speech strongly opposing the legislation. He was one
of the leaders of the 'patriotic' party which wished to retain
Scotland's independence and in 1708 he was imprisoned on
suspicion of supporting a Jacobite rebellion. Portraits of his
father and mother hang nearby in the Private Drawing Room
(see nos.1, 10, 13). The original portrait was painted in about
1706. PG1553

17 George Jamesone 1589/90–1644
*Anne Erskine, Countess of Rothes d.1640, with her
Daughters, Lady Mary Leslie b.1620 (later wife of the 7th
Earl of Eglinton) and Lady Margaret Leslie 1621–88
(later wife of the 2nd Earl of Wemyss)*
oil on canvas, 219.4 × 135.5 cm

This triple portrait of Anne Erskine, who married the 6th Earl
of Rothes, and her daughters Margaret and Mary, was painted
as a companion to a full-length picture of her husband. The
painting, which is signed and dated 1626, was heavily restored
and reworked in the nineteenth century, especially in the faces
of the sitters. However, the picture provides valuable evidence
of costume and jewellery styles as well as providing an early
glimpse of a Scottish interior. PG2456

18 David Scougall fl.1654–77
Marion Hay of Balhousie d.1663
oil on canvas, 72 × 62 cm

The sitter was the wife of George Hay of Balhousie. David
Scougall was the leading portraitist in Scotland at this period.
His only signed painting, *Lady Jean Campbell* (Scottish
National Portrait Gallery), is dated 1654. From that portrait his
oeuvre has been established. He is sometimes referred to as 'Old
Scougall', to differentiate him from his son or nephew John
Scougall (c.1645–1737). *On loan from the Rt Hon the Earl of
Kinnoull to the Scottish National Portrait Gallery.* PGL362

19 David Martin 1737–98
Elizabeth Knox, Mrs Andrew Duncan d.1839
oil on canvas, 74.8 × 63 cm

The sitter was wife of Andrew Duncan (1744–1828) who was
President of the Royal Medical Society and of the Royal College
of Physicians. PG166

20 Attributed to Andrew Allan d.1740
Sir Walter Pringle, Lord Newhall c.1664–1736
oil on canvas, 74.3 × 61.2 cm

The portrait of this Lord of Session was probably painted
around 1730. The portrait painter Andrew Allan (or Allen)
worked in Edinburgh. PG2174

21 Samuel Drummond 1765–1844
Sir David Dundas 1735–1820
oil on canvas, 75.9 × 63.3 cm

The son of an Edinburgh merchant, Dundas saw service in the
Low Countries, Germany and the West Indies. He was famous
for his writings on military tactics and organisation. The artist,
Samuel Drummond, was born in London. He studied at the
Royal Academy, of which he was elected an Associate in 1808,
and where he later became curator of the painting school. He
painted portraits and historical subjects. PG1281

22 Follower of Sir John Baptiste de Medina
*c.*1659–1710
Sir James Murray, Lord Philiphaugh 1655–1708
oil on canvas, 75.2 × 63.3 cm

James Murray sat as a member for Selkirkshire in the conven-
tion of estates in 1678 and was elected Member of Parliament
for the same county in 1670. In 1684 he was arrested on
suspicion of being concerned in the Rye House plot, but,
threatened with torture, he turned King's evidence. After the
Revolution of 1688 he was made an ordinary Lord of Session
and became a close political associate of the 2nd Duke of
Queensberry. In 1702 he was appointed Lord Clerk Register of
Scotland. The artist is unidentified, but was probably an
associate or follower of Sir John Baptiste de Medina. PG948

23 David Martin 1737–98
William Abernethy Drummond 1719/20–1809
oil on canvas, 76.2 × 63.5 cm

The painting is signed and dated 1788. The sitter was a Bishop of
Edinburgh. PG2407

24 Arthur William Devis 1763–1823
Major-General Sir David Ochterlony 1758–1825
oil on canvas, 76.2 × 63.5 cm

The sitter, Sir David Ochterlony, was born in America of Scots
parentage. He had a distinguished military career in the Bengal
Army, culminating in his conquest of Nepal. He then played a
large part in the reconstruction of government in central India.
This portrait was painted in India around 1810. PG2651

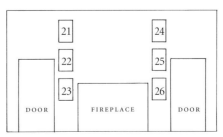

EAST WALL · VESTIBULE

35

25 Attributed to Jeremiah Davison *c.1695–1745*
Duncan Forbes of Culloden 1685–1747
oil on canvas, 76.2 × 63.3 cm

During the Jacobite rising of 1715, Forbes raised forces on behalf of the Government. In 1722 he was MP for the Inverness Burghs, and in 1725 became Lord Advocate. In 1737 he was made Lord President of the Court of Session. When Parliament threatened to punish the City of Edinburgh after the Porteous Riots, Forbes successfully defended the city in Parliament. Both before and during the 1745 Jacobite rising Forbes worked tirelessly for the Government. This portrait is a replica of a painting in Parliament House, Edinburgh. PG545

26 Sir Joshua Reynolds *1723–92*
Sir William Forbes of Pitsligo 1739–1806
oil on canvas, 76.2 × 63.5 cm

Forbes, who was the 6th Baronet of Pitsligo, was recognised as an authority on finance and was consulted by the Prime Minister, William Pitt. In 1781 he purchased back the family lands of Pitsligo, which had been forfeited earlier in the century. There he laid out the village of New Pitsligo and carried out improvements on the estate. He was a prominent member of the Society of Antiquaries of Scotland and played a leading role in Edinburgh life. Sir Joshua Reynolds, as well as his rivals Allan Ramsay and Thomas Gainsborough, were the leading British portraitists of the eighteenth century. PG1296

PASSAGE OFF VESTIBULE

——

1 George Edwin Ewing *1828–84*
Edward, Prince of Wales, later Edward VII 1841–1910
marble, 63.5 cm high

Signed and dated 1868, this bust was probably that exhibited by the artist at the Royal Academy in 1869 (no.1217). Edward VII reigned from 1901 to 1910. *Acquired by the National Galleries of Scotland for Duff House*

2 George Edwin Ewing *1828–84*
Alexandra, Princess of Wales 1844–1925
marble, 58.4 cm high

Signed and dated 1868, this bust was probably that exhibited by the artist at the Royal Academy in 1869 (no.1219). Alexandra married Edward, Prince of Wales in 1863. *Acquired by the National Galleries of Scotland for Duff House*

PRINCE OF WALES'S BEDROOM

———

The Prince of Wales's Bedroom is mainly hung with old master paintings on loan from the National Gallery of Scotland.

SOUTH WINDOW

1 Sir John Steell 1804–91
Queen Victoria 1819–1901
plaster, 56.2 cm high

Queen Victoria reigned from 1837 until her death in 1901. Her grand-daughter, Princess Louise, was the eldest daughter of the Prince of Wales (later Edward VII). As the Princess Royal, she married Alexander, 6th Earl of Fife (later 1st Duke of Fife). This signed artist's plaster, which is dated 1838, is closely related to marble versions, one of which is in the Scottish National Portrait Gallery. PG168

WEST WALL

2 Netherlandish, fifteenth century
The Adoration of the Shepherds
oil on panel, 67.3 × 106.6 cm

This devotional painting has been attributed to various fifteenth-century Netherlandish artists. However, it is likely to have been painted by an artist from the Brussels School, working in the latter part of the century, who may well be Vrancke van der Stockt (*c.*1420–95). The shepherds are shown wearing curious double-fingered mittens, while the spear-like implements they carry were known as 'houlettes', used for throwing stones or earth at a straying sheep to direct it back to the flock. NG1541

3 Netherlandish, sixteenth century
Derick Anthony fl.*1550–69*
oil on panel, 90.5 × 67.4 cm

Derick Anthony was goldsmith to Queen Elizabeth, and some of his work can be seen on the table. The coat of arms depicted in the upper right corner is inscribed *Elizabeth Erley, 1° wife to Derick anthony Margaret Ridge 2° [wife]*. The contemporary inscription notes that the work was painted in 1565, when the sitter was aged forty-three. The painting bears an erroneous inscription identifying the sitter as the *Duke of Chatelherault*. This portrait was thought to be by Antonis Mor (van Dashorst). NG1544

NORTH WALL

4 Isack van Ostade 1621–49
Sportsmen Halting at an Inn
oil on panel, 53.4 × 60.4 cm

This work is signed and dated 1646. Born in Haarlem, Isack was the younger brother of Adriaen van Ostade, who was also his first teacher. Isack preferred to paint more outdoor – and less boorish – scenes than his brother. NG951

5 Imitator of Willem van de Velde the Younger
1633–1707
Ships in a Calm Sea
oil on panel, 36.8 × 49.9 cm

This is painted in the style of the famous Dutch sea painter family, the Van de Velde. Willem was probably a pupil of his father. Both moved to England in around 1672, where they were extremely successful. NG1947

6 Studio of Sir Anthony van Dyck 1599–1641
Marchese Ambrogio Spinola 1569–1630
oil on canvas, 121.9 × 96.5 cm

The sitter was a Genoese general in the service of Spain who served principally in the Spanish-controlled Netherlands. He is shown carrying a baton and wearing the Order of the Golden Fleece. Spinola left the Netherlands at the beginning of 1628, and this portrait has been dated to the previous year. This studio version of the Van Dyck portrait was originally acquired by the National Gallery of Scotland as by Giusto Suttermans. NG87

7 Jan Both *c.*1615–52
Landscape
oil on panel, 44.5 × 54 cm

This landscape with its warm light, ruined buildings and peasants passing through the foreground is typical of the work produced by the Dutch painter Jan Both during his stay in Italy. Born in Utrecht, he and his brother Andries received early

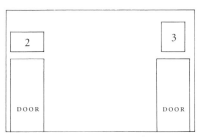

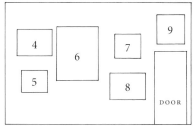

training from their father, a painter on glass, and were afterwards pupils of Abraham Bloemaert. During his stay in Rome, Jan Both was strongly influenced by the paintings of Claude Lorraine. At the end of his life Both returned to Utrecht where he became President of the Guild of Painters. NG912

8 John Fleming 1792–1845
View of Banff with the Bridge over the River Deveron
oil on canvas, 47.1 × 62.9 cm
Acquired by the National Galleries of Scotland for Duff House

9 Florentine, sixteenth century
The Virgin and Child with the Infant St John the Baptist
oil on panel, 87.5 cm circular

This painting, which has been attributed most recently to Francesco Botticini, records the composition of a lost proto-type, and is known through a number of other versions. Its most distinctive feature, which sets it apart from the other versions, is the treatment of the landscape, with its schematic representations of hills and trees. NG645

EAST WALL

10 John Phillip 1817–67
Mary MacKay Caird, later Mrs James Glen 1847–1940
oil on canvas, 105.4 × 80 cm

This portrait of Mrs Glen (née Caird) with her pet dog is signed and dated 1866. The artist, John Phillip, who was born at Oldmeldrum in Aberdeenshire, was sent by Lord Panmure to study at the Royal Academy Schools in London in 1837. He became a member of 'The Clique', which included the artists Augustus Egg, Richard Dadd and W.P. Frith. Phillip became a successful genre painter, specialising in Spanish scenes, thus earning himself the nickname 'Spanish' Phillip. NG2028

11 Aert van der Neer *c.*1603/4–77
Skaters and Kolf Players on a Frozen Waterway
oil on panel, 33.6 × 49 cm

Signed with the artist's monogram, this work was formerly in the Lansdowne collection. *On loan from a Private Collection*

12 Polidoro da Lanciano *c.*1515–65
The Virgin and Sleeping Child
oil on canvas, 53 × 67.3 cm

The design, with the addition of the figure of St Joseph, appears in an engraving of 1660 by Lisabetius, where it was described as being after a painting by Polidoro, then in the collection of Archduke Leopold Wilhelm of Brussels. That painting was the basis of this version, which was at one time considered to be by Titian. NG1931

ANTIQUARIAN CLOSET

────

WEST WALL

1 Lady Isabella Wemyss
The Haunted Beech near Norfolk Farm
pencil on paper, 28.2 × 22.6 cm

This is inscribed as being drawn 'on August 23, 1855 for Mrs S. Erskine'. *Dunimarle loan*

NORTH WALL

2 Sir Francis Grant 1803–78
Sir Walter Scott 1771–1832
oil on canvas, 76.2 × 64 cm

Sir Francis Grant of Kilgraston, later a highly successful society portraitist, painted this, his first important commission, for Lady Ruthven in 1831. The artist worked in Scott's study at Abbotsford, while the writer was occupied in dictating his novel *Count Robert of Paris*, and pursuing his research on demonology. Scott himself was greatly pleased with the picture, and in particular with Grant's portrayal of the two staghounds, Bran and Nimrod. PG103

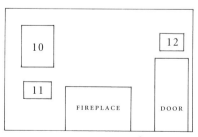

EAST WALL · PRINCE OF WALES'S BEDROOM

GREAT STAIRCASE

—

The great staircase is hung predominantly with old master paintings from the
National Gallery of Scotland and works from the Scottish National Portrait Gallery.

GROUND FLOOR (UNDER STAIRS)

1 Carlo Albacini fl.*c*.1780–1807 and Filippo Albacini 1777–1858 after an unknown Classical sculptor
Epicurus
plaster, 54.5 cm high

For a note on the Albacini busts, see the introduction to the Marble Lobby. NG *loan*

WEST WINDOW

2 Sir John Steell 1804–91
Edward VII 1841–1910
plaster, 71.4 cm high

Edward VII reigned from 1901 to 1910. Steell's plaster bust of his mother, Queen Victoria, is in the Prince of Wales's Bedroom. Steell was the pre-eminent Victorian sculptor in Scotland. The sitter was the father of Princess Louise, Duchess of Fife, who stayed at Duff House. PG169

LOWER NORTH WALL

3 Follower of Jusepe de Ribera 1591–1652
The Martyrdom of St Sebastian
oil on canvas, 202 × 146.5 cm

This painting is influenced by the Spanish-born painter, Jusepe de Ribera, who worked in Naples. The strongly-lit violent treatment of the subject matter is typical of seventeenth-century Neapolitan taste. NG84

4 After an unknown Classical sculptor
Zeus
bronze, 52.5 cm high
Dunimarle loan

5 Follower of Hendrick ter Brugghen *c*.1588–1629
The Beheading of St John the Baptist
oil on canvas, 168 × 218 cm

The uneven quality of this picture suggests it is likely to be a copy of a lost original of *c*.1621. Hendrick ter Brugghen studied with Bloemart in Utrecht before travelling to Rome in 1604. He stayed there for ten years, and became one of the main Dutch exponents of Caravaggio's strongly-lit realist style. The composition is derived from a design for a woodcut by Dürer. NG28

6 Unknown sculptor
Unknown Lady
marble, 43.2 cm high

This white marble bust is on a *Verde di Prato* socle. NG *loan*

7 Philippe Mercier 1689 or 1691–1760
Mrs Dawson
oil on canvas, 90.2 × 67.3 cm

Mercier's portrait of the sitter's husband hangs nearby (see no.12). NG628

LOWER EAST WALL

8 Sir John Baptiste de Medina *c*.1659–1710
Brigadier-General Lord John Hay d.1706
oil on canvas, 126 × 100.5 cm

The sitter, Lord John Hay, was the second son of the 2nd Marquess of Tweeddale. He served in the Royal Scots Dragoons, later known as the Scots Greys, which he commanded in Marlborough's campaign during 1702–3. In 1704 he was made Brigadier-General. Under his command the regiment distinguished itself at Schellenburg and at Ramillies, where it captured the French Regiment du Roi. Lord John Hay died of fever at Courtrai. The artist, Sir John Baptiste de Medina, was born in Brussels of Spanish parentage. He went to London in 1686, but was persuaded by the Earl of Leven and Melville to come to Scotland in 1688, where he became the leading painter of the time. He was knighted in 1707. PG2223

9 Sir Daniel Macnee 1806–82
Louisa Balfour, Mrs James Mackenzie of Craigpath
oil on canvas, 207 × 141 cm

Born at Fintry in Stirlingshire, the artist, Daniel Macnee, received his early training from the landscape painter John Knox. He later established his reputation as a portraitist in both Edinburgh and Glasgow. In 1876 he was elected President of the Royal Scottish Academy. NG1921

10 Unknown sculptor, eighteenth century
Sleeping Cupid
marble, 54.3 cm long

On loan from the Kinnaird Estate, Rossie Priory, to the National Gallery of Scotland

11 Sir John Baptiste de Medina *c*.1659–1710
James Ogilvy, 1st Earl of Seafield 1664–1730
oil on canvas, 125.7 × 103.1 cm

This painting is signed and dated 1695. The sitter, James Ogilvy, was appointed Solicitor-General in 1693, served as Secretary of State from 1696 to 1702 and as Joint-Secretary from 1704 to 1705. He was created Earl of Seafield in 1701 and served as Lord Chancellor of Scotland in 1702–4 and 1705–7. He succeeded his father as 4th Earl of Findlater in 1711. PG1064

12 Philippe Mercier 1689 or 1691–1760
Mr Dawson
oil on canvas, 90.2 × 67.3 cm

This portrait and its companion (no.7) were formerly attributed to William Hogarth. An old inscription describes the sitter as 'Mr. Dawson of Durham', although other labels suggest that he was from Leeds. NG627

13 Grigor Urquhart *c.1797–after 1846*
The Transfiguration (after Raphael)
oil on canvas, 414 × 285 cm

Raphael's most famous painting, which is now in the Picture Gallery of the Vatican, was commissioned in 1516 by Cardinal Giulio de' Medici, cousin and favourite of Pope Leo X. It was produced in competition with Sebastiano del Piombo's altarpiece of the *Raising of Lazarus*, now in the National Gallery, London. This full-size copy was made in Rome during the mid-1820s by the Inverness-born painter Grigor Urquhart. It was bought in 1827 for £300 by the Royal Institution in Edinburgh at the instigation of the painter David Wilkie and the dealer Andrew Wilson. NG66

14 After Giovanni Bellini, *c.1431/6–1516*
The Feast of the Gods
oil on canvas, 174 × 190.5 cm

Mercury, Jupiter, Ceres and Neptune sit in the centre of the painting with Bacchus. On the left Silenus tries to prevent an ass from braying and thereby disturbing Priapus, who is about to surprise the sleeping Vesta. This is a full-size replica of the famous picture by Bellini, which was painted in 1514 for Alfonso d'Este, Duke of Ferrara. Later altered by Dosso Dossi and Titian, that painting is now in the National Gallery of Art, Washington. This copy is of high quality and has been published as a work by Nicolas Poussin. NG458

15 William Aikman 1682–1731
Mrs Erskine of Torrie
oil on canvas, 125.5 × 100 cm

William Aikman was a graduate of Edinburgh University, who became a painter through the encouragement of his uncle Sir John Clerk of Penicuik. After training under Medina in Edinburgh, he studied in London, and later went to Italy. Returning to Britain in 1711, he established himself as a leading portraitist in Edinburgh and London. *Dunimarle loan*

16 John James Napier 1831–82
The First Lesson (The Artist's Wife, Janet Parker Vance Langmuir with their Children, Janet and James)
oil on canvas, 142 × 88.5 cm

Napier was born in Scotland but made his career as a portraitist in London, where he exhibited at the Royal Academy between 1856 and 1876. This lively picture can be dated to *c.*1863. NG2541

17 Attributed to L. Schuneman fl.1651–74
Henry Erskine, 3rd Lord Cardross c.1649–93
oil on canvas, 121 × 96.5 cm

The sitter, Henry Erskine, emigrated to America, where he set up an unsuccessful plantation in North Carolina. Having been driven out by the Spanish, he accompanied the Prince of Orange to England in 1688. In the following year he returned to Scotland, where his estates were restored. He was sworn in as a Privy Councillor and appointed General of the Mint. This little-known painter, who signed his work L. Schuneman, was probably active in Scotland during the later 1660s. PG2206

18 Unknown artist, nineteenth century
Alexander William George Duff, 6th Earl of Fife and 1st Duke of Fife 1849–1912
oil on canvas, 144.2 × 109 cm

After marrying the Princess Louise Victoria Dagmar, the Princess Royal – the eldest daughter of King Edward VII – Alexander, 6th Earl of Fife was created 1st Duke of Fife. He presented Duff House to the town of Banff in 1906. *On loan from the North East of Scotland Museums Service*

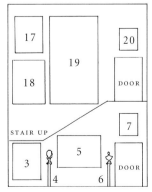

UPPER & LOWER NORTH WALL · GREAT STAIRCASE

19 Sir Henry Raeburn 1756–1823 and Colvin Smith 1795–1875
George Hay, 8th Marquess of Tweeddale 1787–1876
oil on canvas, 302.9 × 206.6 cm

Begun by Raeburn in the final year of his life, this portrait was completed by Colvin Smith, in 1843, for £84. Only the head and torso were completed by Raeburn. The picture until recently hung on the stairs at Yester House, East Lothian. PG2457

20 David Muirhead 1867–1930
Unknown Lady
oil on canvas, 74 × 61.6 cm

Born in Edinburgh, Muirhead started his life as a professional architect, but later studied painting in Edinburgh and London. Recognition came later in life when he was elected an Associate of the Royal Academy in 1928. This portrait is signed and dated 1923. NG1765

UPPER EAST WALL

21 Sir Godfrey Kneller 1646–1723
John Drummond, 1st Earl of Melfort 1649–1714
oil on canvas, 243.7 × 147.2 cm

This portrait, in which Lord Melfort is shown in the robes of Knight of the Thistle, is signed and dated 1688. The sitter, John Drummond, was the second son of James, 3rd Earl of Perth. In 1684 he was appointed Secretary of State for Scotland and was created Earl of Melfort in 1686. Along with his elder brother, he was converted to Roman Catholicism, although probably by political rather than religious arguments. For three years the brothers were virtual rulers of Scotland, exercising considerable influence over James VII and II. The German-born artist Sir Godfrey Kneller was the most prominent court portraitist in London during the late seventeenth and early eighteenth century. PG2746

UPPER SOUTH WALL

22 Philippe Mercier 1689 or 1691–1760
A Girl Knitting
oil on canvas, 76.2 × 63.5 cm

This painting was engraved in mezzotint by J. Watson with the title 'Domestic Employment – Knitting'. A signed version of this genre subject is in a private collection. Philippe Mercier was born in Berlin of French parentage. After studying at the Berlin Academy, he subsequently visited France and Italy. After portraying Frederick, Prince of Wales, son of George II, in Hanover, Mercier became a member of the Prince's household in England. NG434

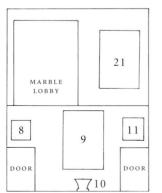

UPPER & LOWER EAST WALL · GREAT STAIRCASE

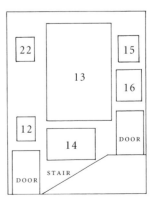

SOUTH WALL · GREAT STAIRCASE

MARBLE LOBBY

———

Painted in simulated Siena marble, the Marble Lobby faithfully copies a decorative scheme devised for the 5th Earl of Fife in the 1860s. This area now contains a series of plaster busts after the Antique, made by Carlo Albacini (fl.c.1780–1807) and Filippo Albacini (1777–1858). These plaster busts were purchased from the Albacini heirs in 1839 by the Scottish landscape painter, Andrew Wilson, for the Trustees Academy in Edinburgh and belong to the National Gallery of Scotland. Others can be seen in the library at Paxton House, Berwickshire and on the North and South staircases at the National Gallery of Scotland. Two more busts can also be seen in the Study off the Outer Library and at the foot of the Great Staircase.

NORTH WALL

1
Vespasian
plaster, 50 cm high
NG loan

2
Plato
plaster, 30 cm high
NG loan

3
Lysias
plaster, 45 cm high
NG loan

4
Plato
plaster, 61 cm high
NG loan

5
Agrippina Minor
plaster, 73 cm high
NG loan

6
Pythagoras
plaster, 49 cm high
NG loan

7
Pindar
plaster, 47 cm high
NG loan

8
Isocrates
plaster, 28 cm high
NG loan

9
Unknown Bearded Man
plaster, 49 cm high
NG loan

EAST WALL

10
Marcus Aurelius
plaster, 91.5 cm high
NG loan

11
Aristotle
plaster, 55 cm high
NG loan

12
Septimius Severus
plaster, 89 cm high
NG loan

SOUTH WALL

13
Julia Sabina
plaster, 76 cm high
NG loan

14
Pupienus
plaster, 73 cm high
NG loan

15
Unknown Bearded Man
plaster, 54 cm high
NG loan

16
Metrodorus and Epicurus
plaster, 53 cm high
NG loan

17
Unknown Bearded Old Man
plaster, 57 cm high
NG loan

18
Valerianus
plaster, 87 cm high
NG loan

19
Unknown Bearded Young Man
plaster, 79 cm high
NG loan

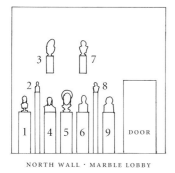

NORTH WALL · MARBLE LOBBY

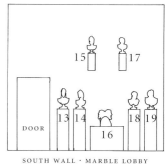

SOUTH WALL · MARBLE LOBBY

NORTH DRAWING ROOM

———

*This room is dominated by a series of portraits by Sir Henry Raeburn,
mainly from the collection of the National Gallery of Scotland. Raeburn was born in Edinburgh
and educated at George Heriot's Hospital. He was apprenticed to the goldsmith James Gilliland,
with whom he painted portrait miniatures, although he later turned to oil painting. At the age of
twenty-four he married a wealthy widow Ann Leslie (née Edgar), who bore him two sons. In 1784
he travelled to Italy, where he spent two years. On returning to Edinburgh, he established a
successful portrait practice, and soon became the leading portrait painter in Scotland. He was
knighted in 1822 by George IV at Hopetoun House and given the vacant post of 'King's Limner in
Scotland'. He painted most of the important figures in the vigorous society that was centred on
Edinburgh at this period, while his style of painting strongly influenced Scottish
portraiture for the rest of the century.*

NORTH WALL

1 Sir John Watson Gordon 1788–1864
Mr Kippen
oil on canvas, 90.2 × 73.7 cm

This work is signed and dated 1810. According to an old
inscription on the back of the canvas, the sitter, Mr Kippen, was
the father of a Mrs Crooks. NG2170

2 Attributed to Sébastien Bourdon 1616–71
The Flight into Egypt
oil on canvas, 58.8 × 70.5 cm

This is an attractive painting from the circle of Sébastien
Bourdon. Born in Montpellier, Bourdon was the son of a glass-
painter. After training in Paris under Jean Barthélemy, he went
to Rome, where he worked as a copyist. Returning a few years
later to Paris, he established himself as a successful history
painter, whose style was highly coloured and influenced by that
of Claude and Poussin. He was one of the twelve artists who, in
1648, founded the Academy of Painting and Sculpture in Paris,
and he was elected one of its rectors from 1655 until his death.
Dunimarle loan

3 Philips Wouverman 1619–68
Soldiers with a Wayside Farrier
oil on panel, 34.8 × 40.9 cm

This painting is signed. Two other works by Wouverman hang
in this room (nos.6 and 14). *Dunimarle loan*

4 John Syme 1795–1861
The Artist's Twin Brothers
oil on canvas, 90.8 × 69.8 cm

Born in Edinburgh, John Syme studied at the Academy of the
Board of Manufactures. He studied flower painting with his
uncle Patrick Syme, before being employed by Raeburn as his
assistant. He was successful as a portraitist and was one of the
original members of the Scottish Academy. This painting was
exhibited at the Edinburgh Exhibition Society in 1816. NG2124

5 David Teniers the Younger 1610–90
A Tavern Interior with Figures Playing Cards
oil on panel, 69.3 × 87.6 cm

This painting is signed. *Dunimarle loan*

6 Philips Wouverman 1619–68
An Army Encampment
oil on panel, 35.2 × 40.6 cm

Wouverman was born in Haarlem and received early lessons
from his father, as well as from Jan Wijnants. After a period in
Hamburg, he returned to Haarlem, where he was received into
the Guild of St Luke. A prolific painter, he specialised in
landscapes filled with horsemen, sometimes involved in
skirmishes or hunts, and peasants and travellers. Two other
works by Wouverman also hang in this room (nos.3 and 14).
Dunimarle loan

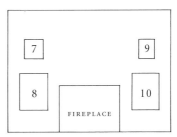

NORTH WALL · NORTH DRAWING ROOM

EAST WALL · NORTH DRAWING ROOM

7 Sir Henry Raeburn 1756–1823
Dr Gardiner 1726–1807
oil on canvas, 89 × 67.5 cm

The sitter was the father of Mrs George Kinnear, whose portrait by Raeburn also belongs to the National Gallery of Scotland. This painting can be dated to around 1806. NG1225

8 Sir Henry Raeburn 1756–1823
Elizabeth Forbes, Mrs Colin Mackenzie of Portmore d.1840
oil on canvas, 126.5 × 100.4 cm

The sitter was the daughter of Sir William Forbes of Pitsligo (see his portrait by Sir Joshua Reynolds in the Vestibule, no.27). Elizabeth Forbes married Colin Mackenzie in 1803. NG2296

9 Sir Henry Raeburn 1756–1823
William Beveridge
oil on canvas, 92.3 × 70 cm

NG1199

10 Sir Henry Raeburn 1756–1823
James Thomson of Nether Bogie 1749–1831
oil on canvas, 127.7 × 101 cm

James Thomson was the son of John Thomson, a merchant in Cupar, and he was admitted Writer to the Signet in 1777. He married Helen, daughter of Patrick Moncrieff of Reidie, Fife, in 1809. NG1923

11 George Jamesone 1589/90–1644
Robert, Mester Erskine
oil on canvas, 230 × 150 cm

The inscription identifies the subject as *Robert, Mester Erskine*, and notes that it was painted in 1627 when the subject was thirty-eight. The artist, whose self-portrait hangs in the Dining Room (no.10), also made a bust-length copy of this signed picture, which is now in a private collection. NG1973

12 After George Engleheart 1753–1829
Lt Col Sir William Erskine 1729–95
oil on panel, 75.3 × 61.3 cm

The artist, George Engleheart, was a noted and prolific miniaturist of the Regency period. Two miniatures by him of this sitter can be seen in the glass case displayed in the China Closet (nos.2 and 3). *Dunimarle loan*

13 After Jan Both c.1615–52
Evening Landscape with Peasants
oil on canvas, 78 × 71.5 cm

Dunimarle loan

14 Philips Wouverman 1619–68
Landscape with Travellers and Shepherds
oil on panel, 33.4 × 46.1 cm

This painting is signed. Two other works by Wouverman hang in this room (nos.3 and 6). *Dunimarle loan*

15 After Meindert Hobbema 1638–1709
Woodland Landscape
oil on canvas, 59.5 × 78.4 cm

Dunimarle loan

16 Scottish, late eighteenth century
Mrs Erskine of Torrie
oil on canvas, 76 × 63.5 cm

This portrait can be dated to just before 1800. *Dunimarle loan*

17 Jacob van Ruisdael c.1628–82
Woodland Landscape with Peasants
oil on canvas, 77.2 × 64.3 cm

This work is signed. Ruisdael, who was born in Haarlem, was the son of Isaack van Ruisdael, a frame-maker, and he studied under Allart van Everdingen. In 1648 he entered the Guild of Haarlem, and in 1659 he settled in Amsterdam. His highly naturalistic landscapes are notable for their solemnity and grandeur. *Dunimarle loan*

18 After Guido Reni 1575–1642
Two Cherubs
oil on canvas, 36 × 46 cm

This work is a fragment from a larger painting. Guido Reni was born at Calvenzano near Bologna. His father, who was a musician, sent him to study under Denys Calvaert, the Antwerp painter, then living in Bologna. He also studied fresco painting under Ferrantini. After moving to Rome, Guido Reni came into contact with the Carracci brothers, whose classical style, together with that of Raphael's work, made a great impact on his own painting. Guido Reni went on to establish himself as one of the most successful painters of the Italian Baroque. *Dunimarle loan*

19 Sir Henry Raeburn 1756–1823
Charlotte Hall, Lady Hume Campbell of Marchmont, and her son, Sir Hugh Hume Campbell of Marchmont, 7th Baronet of Marchmont 1812–1901
oil on canvas, 197 × 151 cm

Charlotte, widow of Anthony Hall, married in 1812 Sir William Hume Campbell of Marchmont, 6th Baronet. The baby is their only child, Sir Hugh Hume Campbell, 7th Baronet, who bequeathed this portrait to the National Gallery of Scotland. NG831

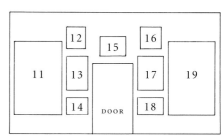

SOUTH WALL · NORTH DRAWING ROOM

20 Mather Brown 1761–1831
Alexander Wedderburn, 1st Earl of Rosslyn 1733–1805
oil on canvas, 127 × 101.9 cm

This portrait was painted in or before 1791. Alexander Wedderburn's career was marked by a search for personal advantage at the expense of political allegiance. In 1770 he at first opposed Prime Minister Lord North's American policy, but soon passed to the latter's side and supported the American war. For this *volte-face* he received the post of Solicitor-General. In 1780 he was appointed Chief Justice with the title of Lord Loughborough. In 1784 he transferred his support to the Whig faction led by Fox, but when he returned to support Pitt he was made Lord Chancellor. Mather Brown was born in America, but came to England and studied under Benjamin West. PG861

21 Sir Henry Raeburn 1756–1823
Zepherina Loughnan, Mrs Henry Veitch of Eliock d.1808
oil on canvas, 123 × 98.4 cm

In 1796 Zepherina Loughnan, married Lieutenant-Colonel Henry Veitch (*d.*1838) of Eliock, near Sanquhar, Dumfriesshire. She was the great granddaughter of Alexander Fergusson of Craigdarroch and of Annie Laurie of Maxwelton. NG2034

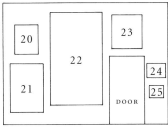

WEST WALL · NORTH DRAWING ROOM

22 Henry William Pickersgill after Sir Henry Raeburn 1756–1823
James Duff, 4th Earl of Fife 1776–1857
oil on canvas, 233.8 × 147.4 cm

A hero of the Peninsular War and a collector of pictures, the 4th Earl was created Baron Fife in the British peerage. The original painting by Raeburn, of which this is a copy, formerly hung at Duff House, and now belongs to Dundee University. *On loan from the North East of Scotland Museums Service*

23 John Michael Wright 1617–94
William Cunningham, 8th Earl of Glencairn c.1610–64
oil on canvas, 127 × 102.2 cm

This portrait was probably painted in 1661. An active Covenanter, Glencairn nonetheless led a rebellion against the Cromwellian occupation of Scotland and after the Restoration was made Lord Chancellor. The painter, one of the most distinctive in British art of the seventeenth century, was trained by George Jamesone in Edinburgh. He later travelled to Rome and worked as antiquary to the Archduke Leopold in the Low Countries. PG2880

24 Aert van der Neer c.1603/4–77
An Evening Lowland Landscape
oil on canvas, 31.5 × 48.5 cm

This work is signed twice. Born at Gorinchen, the painter, Aert van der Neer, moved to Amsterdam, where he had a wine business. He excelled in atmospheric moonlight views. *Dunimarle loan*

25 Dutch, seventeenth century
A Wooded River Landscape with Milkmaid, Cattle and Sheep
oil on panel, 28.3 × 34.9 cm
Dunimarle loan

GREAT DRAWING ROOM

―――――

This room is dominated by six Gobelins tapestries, which are on loan from the Marquess of Zetland.
They were designed by Jacques Nielson (1714–88), with the reserves designed by François Boucher
(1703–70), hanging like simulated framed paintings against grey damask walls. The decorative
sections with flowers and birds (the so-called alentours) were designed by Maurice Jacques (1712–84).
These tapestries were commissioned in 1766 by Sir Lawrence Dundas to hang at his English country
house, Moor Park, Hertfordshire. Similar sets were commissioned, often through the agency of Robert
Adam, for Croome Park, Worcestershire (now in the Metropolitan Museum, New York); Newby Hall,
Yorkshire; Weston Park, Shropshire; and Osterley Park, Middlesex (National Trust).

NORTH WALL

1 François Boucher 1703–70
A Pastoral Scene ('L'Offrande à la Villageoise')
oil on canvas, 231.5 × 91 cm

This composition and the accompanying two pastoral scenes
(nos.3 and 4) come from a set painted for Marchal de Sainci,
économe général du Clergé and one of the great Boucher
collectors, who displayed them at his home in the rue des
Fossés-Montmartre (now the Rue d'Aboukir) in Paris. They
were subsequently acquired by Baron Mayer Amschel de
Rothschild and hung at Mentmore in Buckinghamshire until
they were sold in 1964. This painting, which shows a girl and a
birdcatcher, is signed and dated 1761. It was exhibited at the
Paris Salon in 1765. NG2440

2 Jonathan Richardson 1665–1745
John Carmichael, 3rd Earl of Hyndford 1701–67
oil on canvas, 140.3 × 113.7 cm

Although this portrait is signed and dated 1736, the sitter – then
Lord Carmichael – is shown wearing the uniform of the 3rd
Foot Guards, a regiment in which he served from 1720 to 1734.
He apparently retired from military life at the age of thirty-
three, succeeding to his father's titles three years later. For his
part in negotiating the Treaty of Breslau (1752) between Prussia
and Austria he was made a Knight of the Thistle, and invested
with the order by Frederick the Great. The ribbon and order
may well have been added to the portrait at that later date.
Jonathan Richardson succeeded Sir Godfrey Kneller and
Michael Dahl as one of the most fashionable society portraitists
working in London. PG1556

3 François Boucher 1703–70
A Pastoral Scene ('La Jardinière Endormie')
oil on canvas, 232 × 91 cm

This painting is signed and dated 1762, and was exhibited as part
of a decorative series (nos.1 and 4) at the Paris Salon in 1765.
There it was seen by the great French critic Diderot, who
condemned it: 'Well, my friend, it is at the moment when
Boucher ceases to be painter that he is appointed first painter to
the King.' All three former Marchal de Sainci pictures were later
altered, following criticisms by Diderot. A drawing by Gabriel
de St Aubin of the pictures hanging in the 1765 Salon reveals
that this was originally the largest of these three
paintings. NG2441

EAST WALL

4 François Boucher 1703–70
A Pastoral Scene ('L'Aimable Pastorale')
oil on canvas, 231.5 × 91 cm

This painting is signed and dated 1762. Exhibited at the 1765
Salon, it was condemned by Diderot, 'What abuse of the facility
of the brush'. Like its two companions it was later owned by
Baron Mayer Amschel de Rothschild in the early nineteenth
century. The three pictures were hung at Mentmore, where they
remained until 1964. NG2442

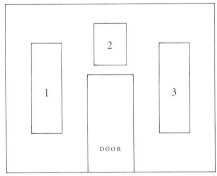

NORTH WALL · GREAT DRAWING ROOM

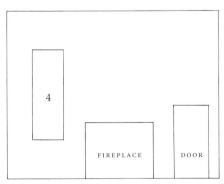

EAST WALL · GREAT DRAWING ROOM

OUTER LIBRARY

—————

The Outer Library is hung with portraits, a number of which depict members of the Stewart dynasty from the fifteenth to the seventeenth centuries. These works are mainly on loan from the Scottish National Portrait Gallery.

WEST WALL

1 Unknown artist, eighteenth century
Colonel John Blackadder 1664–1729
oil on canvas, 114.3 × 96.5 cm

John Blackadder went to Flanders with the Cameronian regiment and took part in most of the sieges and battles of the campaign which ended in the Peace of Ryswick in 1697. He served with the regiment under Marlborough between 1702 and 1709, and became Colonel of this regiment. About 1713 he sold his commission and returned to Scotland. During the Jacobite rising of 1715 he commanded a regiment raised by Glasgow in the government interest. For his services he was appointed deputy governor of Stirling Castle in 1717. PG1534

2 Louis Ferdinand Elle the Elder 1612–89
Sir George Hay, 3rd Earl of Kinnoull d.1650
oil on canvas, 209 × 142 cm

Signed and dated 1649, this portrait represents Sir George Hay, who became the 3rd Earl of Kinnoull, but about whom *The Scots Peerage* in 1908 wrote he 'is not given by the Peerage writers, but there is undoubted evidence for his existence'. He was the son of George, 2nd Earl, and, in turn, was succeeded by his brother William, as 4th Earl. This portrait was painted when the sitter was in France. Louis Ferdinand Elle was from a family of painters, being the son of Ferdinand Elle and father of Louis Ferdinand Elle the Younger. A portraitist and engraver, he was one of the twelve founder members of the Académie in Paris. *On loan from the Rt Hon the Earl of Kinnoull to the Scottish National Portrait Gallery.* PGL359

3 Unknown artist, seventeenth century
General Sir James Lumsden c.1598–c.1660
oil on canvas, 127.3 × 102 cm

James Lumsden as a young man sought his fortune abroad and, with his two brothers, took service with the Swedish king, Gustavus Adolphus, whose miniature portrait can be seen in this portrait hanging from a chain around his neck. Lumsden served with distinction in Germany during the Thirty Years War and attained the rank of Colonel, commanding a regiment of Scots. The artist has not been identified, but as there are a number of similar portraits of officers of various nationalities who served in the Swedish army, he was probably a Swede or a German. *On loan from Miss Sandys-Lumsdaine to the Scottish National Portrait Gallery.* PGL275

4 John Scougall c.1645–1737 after an unknown sixteenth-century artist
John Erskine, 1st Earl of Mar d.1572
oil on canvas, 73.7 × 60.7 cm

The sitter, John Erskine, who had taken minor orders, returned to a secular life and renounced all his preferments when, his two elder brothers dying before his father, he succeeded as 6th Lord Erskine. As Commander of Edinburgh Castle he received Mary of Guise, the Queen Regent, into the castle during her last illness. John Erskine was created Earl of Mar by Mary, Queen of Scots in 1565. He served in the Government and took over the Regency after the death of the Earl of Lennox in 1571. He was also made guardian of the infant James VI and was responsible for his early upbringing. John Scougall was a member of the family of painters, who were active in Scotland during the second half of the seventeenth century and the early eighteenth century. PG653

NORTH WALL

5 After Sir Peter Lely 1618–80
Charles I 1600–49 and James, Duke of York, later James VII and II, 1633–1701
oil on canvas, 103.5 × 140.3 cm

This is a near contemporary copy of the portrait painted by Sir Peter Lely during the King's detention at Hampton Court in 1647. The original picture was painted for the 10th Earl of Northumberland in whose charge the children of the King had been placed. Sir Peter Lely was born at Soest near Amersfoort, near Utrecht. After studying in Haarlem, he came to England in 1641 and was introduced to Charles I in 1647. Later Lely portrayed Cromwell and enjoyed considerable private practice under him. He was particularly favoured by Charles II, and painted a famous series of portraits of the beauties of his court. He was knighted in 1679. PG858

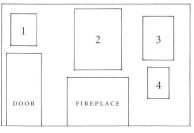

WEST WALL · OUTER LIBRARY

6 Netherlandish, sixteenth century
Unknown Gentleman (called James IV)
oil on panel, 36.5 × 29.3 cm

When acquired, this painting was attributed to Holbein. However it is closer to the work of Joos van Cleve or Quinten Metsys, and probably painted in Antwerp during the second decade of the sixteenth century. By around 1720 it was in the Lothian collection at Newbattle Abbey, where it was paired with a portrait of a similar size, then thought to depict James's Queen, Margaret Tudor, also believed to be by Holbein. There is a copy of this painting in the series of historical portraits by George Jamesone at Newbattle. NG1929

7 Unknown artist, sixteenth century
James I 1394–1437
oil on panel, 37.5 × 24.7 cm

James I reigned as King of Scots from 1406 to 1437. He was the third son of Robert III and third of the Stewart Kings. He was assassinated in Perth by a group of conspirators led by Sir Robert Graham. He married Joan, daughter of the 1st Earl of Somerset, and was succeeded by his six-year-old son, James II. This portrait is one of a set depicting the Stewart kings. The artist is unknown but it is the work of an unidentified Scottish painter of the mid-sixteenth century, and is probably based on an earlier portrait, now lost. PG337

8 Unknown artist, seventeenth century
Charles I 1600–49
oil on canvas, 35.4 × 26.2 cm

The second son of James VI and Anne of Denmark, Charles was created Prince of Wales in 1616 after the death of his brother Henry in 1612. He succeeded to the throne in 1625 and was married in the same year to Princess Henrietta Maria of France. From the beginning of his reign Charles was in conflict with the House of Commons in England, and with the Presbyterians in Scotland. After the Civil War and during his period of captivity, when he managed to carry on intrigues with a view to recovering power, he was brought to trial, condemned and executed. Charles was a great patron of the arts; not only did he amass a magnificent collection of pictures by Old Masters such as Raphael and Titian, but he also patronised many contemporary artists, the most important being Bernini, Rubens and Van Dyck. PG1454

9 Unknown artist, sixteenth century
James V 1512–42
oil on panel, 49.5 × 31.1 cm

James V, who succeeded to the throne when only an infant, reigned as King of Scots from 1513 to 1542. As in the previous reigns, during the King's minority, the country was torn by the feuds of the nobles intent on seizing power for themselves. During this period James was mainly controlled by the Douglas family until he assumed the throne in 1528. After war broke out with England, the Scots suffered a severe defeat at Solway Moss in 1542. About three weeks later, a few days after the birth of his daughter and heir, Mary, James died at Falkland Palace. The artist is unknown but it is the work of an unidentified Scottish painter of the mid-sixteenth century, and is probably based on an earlier portrait, now lost. PG338

10 After Sir Anthony van Dyck 1599–1641
George Gordon, 2nd Marquess of Huntly c.1592–1649
oil on canvas, 58.3 × 44.5 cm

This portrait is based on the full-length of around 1638 by Van Dyck in the collection of the Duke of Buccleuch at Bowhill. In 1623, the sitter, George Gordon, commanded a Scots company in France, returning to Scotland in 1636 on the death of his father. In the struggle that ensued in the following years between King and Covenanters, Huntly sided with King Charles. In the north he was opposed by Montrose; he was betrayed into his enemies' hands and was taken to Edinburgh. Freed in 1639, Huntly went to England for a period but was back in Scotland by 1643, when he gave his support to Montrose, now acting on the Royalist side. Driven by Argyll to take refuge in Caithness, Huntly subsequently came South and stormed the town of Aberdeen in 1645. He was captured in 1649 and after being tried on a charge of treason he was beheaded at the Mercat Cross. PG902

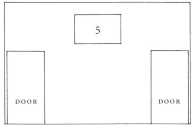

NORTH WALL · OUTER LIBRARY

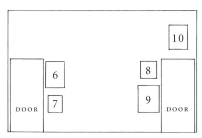

EAST WALL · OUTER LIBRARY

11 Unknown artist, seventeenth century
Mary, Queen of Scots 1542–87
oil on panel, 25.2 × 20 cm

Mary, Queen of Scots, reigned as monarch from 1542 to 1567. It has been said that 'no historical personage outside Scripture is better known to the world at large than Mary Stewart. Historians, poets and romancers of every country have striven to paint, to analyse, and to explain her character and her fortunes as a woman and a queen'. Active rebellion finally drove her to seek refuge in England, where she was imprisoned by Queen Elizabeth. Mary was considered rightful Queen of England and Scotland by Roman Catholics and her existence constituted a continual threat to Elizabeth. Finally, after Mary had become implicated in a plot to assassinate Elizabeth, she was tried, condemned and executed at Fotheringhay in 1587. PG130

12 Hugh Monro after an unknown artist
James Stewart, Earl of Moray c.1531–70
oil on canvas, 38 × 28 cm

The sitter, James Stewart, was the natural son of King James V and Margaret, daughter of Lord Erskine. He was educated at St Andrews and accompanied his half sister Mary when she went to France in 1548. Later he took an active part in the civil war in Scotland between the reformers and the adherents of the old faith led by Mary of Guise, widow of James V and Regent of Scotland. When Mary, Queen of Scots returned to assume the throne Moray supported her, but opposed her church policy which favoured the Roman Catholics. Moray accepted the Regency after Mary's abdication in 1567, and commanded the army which defeated her at Langside. He ruled Scotland with great ability until his assassination by James Hamilton of Bothwellhaugh in 1570. This picture is a modern copy of the portrait by an unknown artist in the Palace of Holyroodhouse. It was commissioned by the Scottish National Portrait Gallery in 1925. PG1002

13 French, seventeenth century
Venus de' Medici
bronze, 71.5 cm high

A copy of the famous classical statue, carved from marble, in the Galleria degli Uffizi, Florence, this bronze is stamped with a mark indicating its provenance from the French Royal collection. It may be by the important French sculptor, François Girardon (1628–1715). *Dunimarle loan*

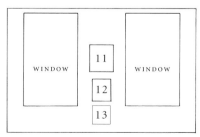

SOUTH WALL · OUTER LIBRARY

STUDY OFF OUTER LIBRARY

*The Study off the Outer Library is hung with works on paper,
including prints, drawings and watercolours.*

1 Carlo Albacini fl.*c.*1780–1807 and Filippo Albacini
1777–1858 after an unknown Roman sculptor
Theocritus
plaster, 74.5 cm high
NG *loan*

NORTH WALL

2 Robert Price 1717–61
Troup Head
grey wash, 24.6 × 37.8 cm
Troup Head is near Banff and Macduff. *Acquired by the
National Galleries of Scotland for Duff House.* NG D5191

3 Robert Price 1717–61
Duff House and the Town of Banff
grey wash, 24.8 × 38.5 cm
*Acquired by the National Galleries of Scotland for Duff
House.* NG D5192

4 William Faithorn after John Preston Neale fl.*c.*1831
Duff House, Banffshire
line engraving, 11.8 × 14.5 cm
*Acquired by the National Galleries of Scotland for Duff
House.* NG P2886

5 J. Walker after James Moore
Duff House, Banffshire
line engraving, 14.5 × 10.5 cm
On loan from the Duke of Fife.

EAST WALL

6 Carlo Albacini fl.*c.*1780–1807 and Filippo Albacini
1777–1858 after an unknown Roman sculptor
Aeschines
plaster, 73.4 cm high
NG *loan*

7 William Daniell 1769–1837
Duff House
coloured aquatint, 23 × 30 cm
This was published in 1822. *Acquired by the National Galleries of
Scotland for Duff House.*

8 William Daniell 1769–1837
Duff House
aquatint, 23 × 30 cm
This was published in 1822. *Acquired by the National Galleries of
Scotland for Duff House.*

SOUTH WALL

9 Edward Burton after Colvin Smith 1795–1875
Captain John Grant of Congash fl.1848
mezzotint, 30.4 × 37.8 cm
The sitter was factor to the then Earl of Seafield. S.P.V.112.1

9 William Holl after Sir Henry Raeburn 1756–1823
James Duff, 4th Earl of Fife 1776–1857
stipple, 32.8 × 25.3 cm
Pickersgill's copy of Raeburn's original full-length of this sitter,
hangs nearby in the North Drawing Room (see no.22).
S.P.VI.242.1

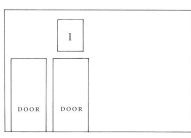

SOUTH WALL · INNER LIBRARY

INNER LIBRARY

―――――

The Inner Library is mainly hung with Jacobite portraits from the eighteenth century, which are on loan from the Scottish National Portrait Gallery.

SOUTH WALL

1 Attributed to Domenico Dupra 1689–1770
Sir James Steuart 1713–80
oil on canvas, 127.3 × 98 cm

Sir James Steuart, 3rd Baronet (1713–80) was one of the most important political economists of the eighteenth century. Domenico Dupra painted a number of important portraits of the Jacobite court in exile at Rome. PG2853

WEST WALL

2 After Louis-Gabriel Blanchet 1705–72
Princess Maria Clementina Sobieska 1702–35
oil on canvas, 76.5 × 63.7 cm

Consort of Prince James Francis Edward Stewart, Princess Maria Clementina was the daughter of Prince James Sobieska, eldest son of King John of Poland. Her marriage to the 'Old Pretender' took place at Montefiascone on 1 September 1719, when she was 17 years of age. Princess Clementina was the mother of Prince Charles Edward Stewart and Prince Henry Benedict Stewart. She retired in seclusion to a convent six months after the birth of her younger son, and remained there until eight years before her death. Blanchet was a French painter who worked in Italy and was patronised by the exiled House of Stewart. PG1837

3 Unknown artist, eighteenth century
Prince James Francis Edward Stewart 1688–1776
oil on canvas, 76.2 × 62.9 cm

Prince James, the only son of James VII and II and Mary of Modena, was secretly conveyed to France with his mother during the Revolution of 1688. At his father's death in 1701 he was proclaimed King of Great Britain at the French court, and was considered King James VIII and III by the Jacobites. He married Princess Clementina Sobieska who bore him two sons, Prince Charles and Prince Henry. A great number of portraits were painted of James at all stages of his career, as gifts for his supporters both at home and abroad. PG305

NORTH WALL

4 After Allan Ramsay 1713–84
Flora Macdonald 1722–90
oil on canvas, 76.7 × 64.2 cm

This famous Jacobite heroine was the daughter of Ranald Macdonald, a farmer at Milton on the island of South Uist in the Hebrides. In 1746, while on a visit to the Clanranalds, who lived on the neighbouring island of Benbecula, she met Prince Charles Edward Stewart in flight after the Battle of Culloden. She helped the Prince to reach Skye, but was subsequently imprisoned in the Tower of London after the Prince's escape. The original version of this portrait, which was painted in London during 1749, is now in the Ashmolean Museum, Oxford. PG947

5 Unknown artist, eighteenth century
Princess Louisa of Stolberg 1753–1824
oil on canvas, 56.4 × 43.3 cm

The sitter was wife of Prince Charles Edward Stewart. PG1520

6 After Cornelius Cure fl.*c.*1574–*c.*1609
and William Cure fl.*c.*1605–32
Mary, Queen of Scots 1542–87
electrotype bust, 64.6 cm high

Mary, Queen of Scots reigned from 1542 to 1567. Imprisoned by Queen Elizabeth, she was tried, condemned and executed at Fotheringhay in 1587. This bust is a nineteenth-century copy taken from the monument to Mary, which was designed and built in 1606 by Cornelius Cure and his son William, in Westminster Abbey. The portrait was probably based on a portrait miniature by Nicholas Hilliard. PG151

7 William Delacour fl.1740–67
Sir Stuart Threipland 1716–1805
oil on canvas, 130 × 152.5 cm

The sitter, who was a physician and an ardent supporter of Prince Charles Edward Stewart, is shown wearing the Highland dress he wore at the Battle of Culloden in 1746, an event which is signified by the allegorical and military details within the picture. Sir Stuart Threipland became *de jure* 3rd Baronet after the death of his father in 1746. William Delacour was a portraitist and landscape painter. Born in France, he worked in London and Dublin, before settling in Edinburgh by 1757, where he stayed for the rest of his life. He painted decorative landscapes for a number of the houses designed by John and Robert Adam. In 1760 he was appointed the first Master of the Trustees' Academy in Edinburgh. *On loan from Mark Murray Threipland to the Scottish National Portrait Gallery.* PGL354

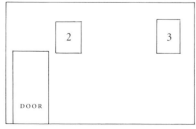

WEST WALL · INNER LIBRARY

8 Unknown artist, eighteenth century
Prince Charles Edward Stewart 1720–88
oil on canvas, 76.2 × 63.8 cm

Prince Charles, the elder son of Prince James Francis Edward, was born and brought up in Rome. In 1745 he sailed for Scotland and landed in the Hebrides with only a few followers in an unsuccessful attempt to reclaim the throne for his father. In April 1746 Prince Charles's army was totally defeated and dispersed by the Government forces under the Duke of Cumberland at the Battle of Culloden. After a period of hiding in the Western Highlands, Charles escaped to France and remained in exile for the rest of his life. In 1772 he married Princess Louisa of Stolberg, by whom he had no children; his brother Henry Benedict was therefore considered by the Jacobites to be next in line of succession. In 1753 he had an illegitimate daughter, Charlotte, by his mistress Clementina Walkinshaw, whom he created Duchess of Albany. PG1510

EAST WALL

9 After Sir Joshua Reynolds 1723–92
William Augustus, Duke of Cumberland 1721–65
oil on canvas, 76.2 × 63.5 cm

The sitter was the third son of George II. He commanded the Hanoverian force, which defeated Prince Charles Edward Stewart at the Battle of Culloden in 1746. Afterwards his forces hunted down the Jacobites with great severity, and he became known as 'Butcher' Cumberland. Sir Joshua Reynolds was born at Plympton in Devon, and studied in London under Hudson and later in Italy. On the foundation of the Royal Academy in 1768, Reynolds became its first President. PG910

10 Unknown tartan-maker, eighteenth century
Pieces of Tartan
tartan, 43.2 × 43.2 cm

The original piece of tartan, from which these fragments are alleged to come, was considered to have been given to Prince Charles Edward Stewart by Susanna Kennedy, Countess of Eglinton. According to an inscription on the frame this tartan was worn by the Prince in Edinburgh during September 1745. *Dunimarle loan*

CAFÉ

———

This is hung with twelve prints by Francesco Rossini showing views of Rome, which were published there between 1819 and 1822. Dunimarle loan

1 *View of the Quirinal Hill (Veduta Generale del Monte Quirinale)*

2 *View of the Pantheon of Agrippa (Veduta del Pantheon di Agrippa)*

3 *The Inside of the Colosseum (Interno del Colosseo)*

4 *View of the Pantheon of Agrippa (Veduta del Pantheon di Agrippa)*

5 *View of the Pyramid of C. Sestius (Veduta del Piramide di C. Sestio)*

6 *In Front of the Temple of Jupiter Statore (Avanzi del Tempio di Giove Statore)*

7 *In Front of the Temple of Concordia (Avanzi del Tempio della Concordia)*

8 *View of the Roman Forum (Veduta generale del Foro Romano)*

9 *View of the Amphitheatre of Flavius, called the Colosseum (Veduta del Anfiteatro Flavio, detto il Colosseo)*

10 *View of the Inside of the Pronaos of the Pantheon (Veduta del Interno del Pronao del Pantheon)*

11 *The Gran Mola of Hadrian and the Bridge of Elius (Veduta della Gran Mola Adriana e Ponte Elio)*

12 *The Arch of Septimius, Rome (Veduta del Arco di Settimio)*

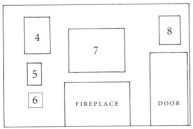

NORTH WALL · INNER LIBRARY

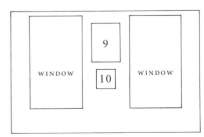

EAST WALL · INNER LIBRARY

BACK STAIRCASE

———

*The following ten watercolours are copies of Spanish Old Master
paintings. They were copied for William Stirling of Keir, later Sir William Stirling-
Maxwell, 9th Baronet (1818–78) and were all bought recently by the National Gallery of
Scotland from the sale held in 1995 of items from Keir House, Dunblane. The first three
watercolours are still in their original mid-nineteenth-century frames, which are
surmounted with seven-starred crowns. These were designed by Stirling-Maxwell and made
from timber on his estate at Keir. Stirling-Maxwell was a great collector of Spanish
paintings and wrote widely on Spanish art. Much of his collection of Spanish pictures
can be seen at Pollok House (National Trust for Scotland) in Glasgow.*

1 Joseph West *b*.1797 after Alonso Cano 1601–67
The Virgin on a Cloud of Cherubs
watercolour on paper, 34.2 × 22.8 cm
The painting by Cano was copied in 1857. NG D5404A

2 Joseph West *b*.1797 after Jusepe de Ribera 1591–1652
Assumption of the Virgin
watercolour on paper, 34.2 × 22.8 cm
This watercolour was copied in 1857. NG D5404C

3 Joseph West *b*.1797 after Bartolomé Esteban Murillo
1618–82
The Virgin and Child Seated
watercolour on paper, 34.2 × 22.8 cm
The painting by Murillo was copied in 1857. NG D5404

4 Joseph West *b*.1797
after Diego Velázquez 1599–1660
The Spinners
watercolour on paper, 26.6 × 33 cm
This watercolour copy was made in 1849. The original painting
is now in the Museo del Prado, Madrid. NG D5406A

5 Joseph West *b*.1797
after Diego Velázquez 1599–1660
*Justin of Nassau Surrendering the Keys of Breda to
Ambrosio Spinola, June 1625*
watercolour on paper, 26.2 × 32.5 cm
This watercolour copy was made in 1849. The original painting
is now in the Museo del Prado, Madrid. NG D5406B

6 Joseph West *b*.1797
after Bartolomé Esteban Murillo 1618–82
The Release of St Peter
watercolour on paper, 28.9 × 31.5 cm
This watercolour was painted in 1853. The original painting is
now in the Hermitage Museum, St Petersburg. NG D5407C

7 Joseph West *b*.1797
after Bartolomé Esteban Murillo 1618–82
The Pool of Bethesda
watercolour on paper, 30.5 × 31.1 cm
This watercolour was painted in 1853, when the original
painting belonged to Mr G. Tomline at Carlton House Terrace
in London. NG D5407B

8 Joseph West *b*.1797
after Bartolomé Esteban Murillo 1618–82
The Prodigal Son
watercolour on paper, 29.5 × 31.4 cm
This watercolour was painted in 1851, when the original
painting belonged to the Duke of Sutherland in London.
NG D5407A

9 Joseph West *b*.1797
after Bartolomé Esteban Murillo 1618–82
Abraham
watercolour on paper, 30.5 × 32 cm
At the time this watercolour copy was made in 1851, the original
painting belonged to the Duke of Sutherland in London. NG
D5405B

10 Joseph West *b*.1797 after Diego Velázquez
1599–1660
Joseph's Coat
watercolour on paper, 27.8 × 35.5 cm
The painting, which is in the Escorial Palace outside Madrid,
was copied in 1852. NG D5405A

INDEX OF ARTISTS

━━━

INDEX OF SITTERS

―――

FURTHER READING

Sir William Musgrave, 'Painted Portraits in Duff-House', 1796 [from the 'Lists' of painted portraits of distinguished persons in various Public Buildings and Capital Mansions in England and Scotland], British Museum, London, BM Add. MS. 6391/2

[James, 2nd Earl of Fife], *Catalogue of the Portraits & Pictures in the different Houses belonging to James Earl of Fife*, London 1807 (1st edn 1798)

J. T., *Dunimarle*, 2nd edn, Dunfermline 1873

K. Warren Clouston and M. Crosby Smith, 'The Duke of Fife's Collection at Duff House', Part I, *The Connoisseur*, x, no.37, September 1904, pp.3–9, and Part II, *op. cit.*, x, no.38, pp.67–74

Catalogue of Pictures by Old Masters and Historical Portraits the property of His Grace the Duke of Fife, KT *removed from Duff House, Banffshire, which His Grace recently presented to the neighbouring community. These Pictures are part of a very large Collection which was made by James, Earl of Fife, towards the end of the Eighteenth Century, and were placed in Duff House, where they have remained ever since*, Christie's, London, 7 June 1907

Canon James Harper, 'Catalogue Raisonné of the Erskine of Torrie Institute drawn up by the Revnd. Canon Harper M.A. Curator and Chaplain of St Serf's – Dunimarle 1912', unpublished MS, Mrs Magdalene Sharpe Erskine's Trust, Dunimarle Castle, Culross, Fife

National Gallery of Scotland: Catalogue of Paintings and Sculpture, Edinburgh 1957

Rupert Gunnis, *Dictionary of British Sculptors 1660–1851*, rev edn, London 1968 (1st edn 1953)

Colin Thompson and Hugh Brigstocke, *National Gallery of Scotland: Shorter Catalogue*, Edinburgh 1970

Painting in Scotland 1570–1650, exh. cat., Duncan Thomson (ed), Scottish National Portrait Gallery, Edinburgh 1975

National Gallery of Scotland: Illustrations, Edinburgh 1980

The Torrie Collection: An Exhibition to mark the Quarter-centenary of the University of Edinburgh, exh. cat., Duncan Macmillan (ed), The Talbot Rice Art Centre, University of Edinburgh, 1983

A. A. Tait, *Duff House*, Edinburgh [1986]

Patrons and Painters: Art in Scotland 1650–1760, exh. cat., James Holloway (ed), Scottish National Portrait Gallery, Edinburgh 1989

Helen Smailes, *The Concise Catalogue of the Scottish National Portrait Gallery*, Edinburgh 1990

Helen Smailes, 'A history of the Statue Gallery at the Trustees' Academy in Edinburgh and the acquisition of the Albacini casts in 1838', *Journal of the History of Collections*, III, no.2, 1991, pp.125–43

Dutch Art and Scotland: A Reflection of Taste, exh. cat., Julia Lloyd Williams (ed), National Gallery of Scotland, Edinburgh 1992

Allan Ramsay 1713–1784, exh. cat., Alastair Smart (ed), Scottish National Portrait Gallery, Edinburgh and National Portrait Gallery, London 1992–3

Hugh Brigstocke, *Italian and Spanish Paintings in the National Gallery of Scotland*, 2nd edn, Edinburgh 1993 (1st edn, 1978)

Timothy Clifford and Ian Gow, *Duff House*, Edinburgh 1995

John Cornforth, 'Duff House, Banffshire: a property in the guardianship of Historic Scotland', *Country Life*, 21 September 1995, pp.66–71

The Dictionary of Art, Jane Turner (ed), 34 vols, London 1996

The National Gallery of Scotland, Concise Catalogue of the Paintings, Edinburgh 1997

Raeburn, exh. cat., Duncan Thomson (ed), Royal Scottish Academy, Edinburgh and National Portrait Gallery, London, 1997–8